Third-Party Risk Management
Complete Self-Assessment Guide

The guidance in this Self-Assessment is based on Third-Party Risk Management best practices and standards in business process architecture, design and quality management. The guidance is also based on the professional judgment of the individual collaborators listed in the Acknowledgments.

Notice of rights

You are licensed to use the Self-Assessment contents in your presentations and materials for internal use and customers without asking us - we are here to help.

Trademarks

Copyright © by The Art of Service
http://theartofservice.com
service@theartofservice.com

D0911733

Table of Contents

About The Art of Service

The Art of Service, Business Process Architects since 2000, is dedicated to helping stakeholders achieve excellence.

Defining, designing, creating, and implementing a process to solve a stakeholders challenge or meet an objective is the most valuable role… In EVERY group, company, organization and department.

Unless you're talking a one-time, single-use project, there should be a process. Whether that process is managed and implemented by humans, AI, or a combination of the two, it needs to be designed by someone with a complex enough perspective to ask the right questions.

Someone capable of asking the right questions and step back and say, 'What are we really trying to accomplish here? And is there a different way to look at it?'

With The Art of Service's Standard Requirements Self-Assessments, we empower people who can do just that — whether their title is marketer, entrepreneur, manager, salesperson, consultant, Business Process Manager, executive assistant, IT Manager, CIO etc... —they are the people who rule the future. They are people who watch the process as it happens, and ask the right questions to make the process work better.

Contact us when you need any support with this Self-Assessment and any help with templates, blue-prints and examples of standard documents you might need:

http://theartofservice.com
service@theartofservice.com

Acknowledgments

This checklist was developed under the auspices of The Art of Service, chaired by Gerardus Blokdyk.

Representatives from several client companies participated in the preparation of this Self-Assessment.

Our deepest gratitude goes out to Matt Champagne, Ph.D. Surveys Expert, for his invaluable help and advise in structuring the Self Assessment.

Mr Champagne can be contacted at http://matthewchampagne.com/

In addition, we are thankful for the design and printing services provided.

Included Resources - how to access

Included with your purchase of the book is the Third-Party Risk Management Self-Assessment Spreadsheet Dashboard which contains all questions and Self-Assessment areas and auto-generates insights, graphs, and project RACI planning - all with examples to get you started right away.

Get it now- you will be glad you did - do it now, before you forget.

How? Simply send an email to **access@theartofservice.com** with this books' title in the subject to get the Third-Party Risk Management Self Assessment Tool right away.

Your feedback is invaluable to us

If you recently bought this book, we would love to hear from you! You can do this by writing a review on amazon (or the online store where you purchased this book) about your last purchase! As part of our continual service improvement process, we love to hear real client experiences and feedback.

How does it work?
To post a review on Amazon, just log in to your account and click on the Create Your Own Review button (under Customer Reviews) of the relevant product page. You can find examples of product reviews in Amazon. If you purchased from another online store, simply follow their procedures.

What happens when I submit my review?
Once you have submitted your review, send us an email at review@theartofservice.com with the link to your review so we can properly thank you for your feedback.

Purpose of this Self-Assessment

This Self-Assessment has been developed to improve understanding of the requirements and elements of Third-Party Risk Management, based on best practices and standards in business process architecture, design and quality management.

It is designed to allow for a rapid Self-Assessment to determine how closely existing management practices and procedures correspond to the elements of the Self-Assessment.

The criteria of requirements and elements of Third-Party Risk Management have been rephrased in the format of a Self-Assessment questionnaire, with a seven-criterion scoring system, as explained in this document.

In this format, even with limited background knowledge of Third-Party Risk Management, a manager can quickly review existing operations to determine how they measure up to the standards. This in turn can serve as the starting point of a 'gap analysis' to identify management tools or system elements that might usefully be implemented in the organization to help improve overall performance.

How to use the Self-Assessment

On the following pages are a series of questions to identify to what extent your Third-Party Risk Management initiative is complete in comparison to the requirements set in standards.

To facilitate answering the questions, there is a space in front of each question to enter a score on a scale of '1' to '5'.

1 Strongly Disagree

2 Disagree

3 Neutral

4 Agree

5 Strongly Agree

Read the question and rate it with the following in front of mind:

'In my belief, the answer to this question is clearly defined'.

There are two ways in which you can choose to interpret this statement;
1.   how aware are you that the answer to the question is clearly defined
2.   for more in-depth analysis you can choose to gather evidence and confirm the answer to the question. This

obviously will take more time, most Self-Assessment users opt for the first way to interpret the question and dig deeper later on based on the outcome of the overall Self-Assessment.

A score of '1' would mean that the answer is not clear at all, where a '5' would mean the answer is crystal clear and defined. Leave emtpy when the question is not applicable or you don't want to answer it, you can skip it without affecting your score. Write your score in the space provided.

After you have responded to all the appropriate statements in each section, compute your average score for that section, using the formula provided, and round to the nearest tenth. Then transfer to the corresponding spoke in the Third-Party Risk Management Scorecard on the second next page of the Self-Assessment.

Your completed Third-Party Risk Management Scorecard will give you a clear presentation of which Third-Party Risk Management areas need attention.

Third-Party Risk Management Scorecard Example

Example of how the finalized Scorecard can look like:

Third-Party Risk Management Scorecard

Your Scores:

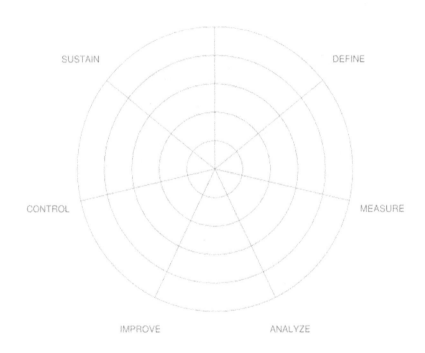

BEGINNING OF THE SELF-ASSESSMENT:

CRITERION #1: RECOGNIZE

INTENT: Be aware of the need for change. Recognize that there is an unfavorable variation, problem or symptom.

In my belief, the answer to this question is clearly defined:

5 Strongly Agree

4 Agree

3 Neutral

2 Disagree

1 Strongly Disagree

1. What would happen if Third-Party Risk Management weren't done?
<--- Score

2. How are the Third-Party Risk Management's objectives aligned to the organization's overall business strategy?
<--- Score

3. Are there any specific expectations or concerns about the Third-Party Risk Management team, Third-Party Risk Management itself?
<--- Score

4. What are the business objectives to be achieved with Third-Party Risk Management?
<--- Score

5. Will new equipment/products be required to facilitate Third-Party Risk Management delivery for example is new software needed?
<--- Score

6. What is the smallest subset of the problem we can usefully solve?
<--- Score

7. Will it solve real problems?
<--- Score

8. Think about the people you identified for your Third-Party Risk Management project and the project responsibilities you would assign to them. what kind of training do you think they would need to perform these responsibilities effectively?
<--- Score

9. Who defines the rules in relation to any given issue?
<--- Score

10. How can auditing be a preventative security measure?
<--- Score

11. What should be considered when identifying

available resources, constraints, and deadlines?
<--- Score

12. As a sponsor, customer or management, how important is it to meet goals, objectives?
<--- Score

13. What does Third-Party Risk Management success mean to the stakeholders?
<--- Score

14. How do you identify the kinds of information that you will need?
<--- Score

15. Does Third-Party Risk Management create potential expectations in other areas that need to be recognized and considered?
<--- Score

16. How are we going to measure success?
<--- Score

17. Are there recognized Third-Party Risk Management problems?
<--- Score

18. What situation(s) led to this Third-Party Risk Management Self Assessment?
<--- Score

19. What is the smallest subset of the problem we can usefully solve?
<--- Score

20. How do you prevent errors and rework?

<--- Score

21. Will Third-Party Risk Management deliverables need to be tested and, if so, by whom?
<--- Score

22. For your Third-Party Risk Management project, identify and describe the business environment. is there more than one layer to the business environment?
<--- Score

23. Are controls defined to recognize and contain problems?
<--- Score

24. How much are sponsors, customers, partners, stakeholders involved in Third-Party Risk Management? In other words, what are the risks, if Third-Party Risk Management does not deliver successfully?
<--- Score

25. Who had the original idea?
<--- Score

26. What training and capacity building actions are needed to implement proposed reforms?
<--- Score

27. What else needs to be measured?
<--- Score

28. Who else hopes to benefit from it?
<--- Score

29. Is it clear when you think of the day ahead of you what activities and tasks you need to complete?

<--- Score

30. Have you identified your Third-Party Risk Management key performance indicators?

<--- Score

31. Who needs to know about Third-Party Risk Management ?

<--- Score

32. Do we know what we need to know about this topic?

<--- Score

33. Why do we need to keep records?

<--- Score

34. When a Third-Party Risk Management manager recognizes a problem, what options are available?

<--- Score

35. How do we Identify specific Third-Party Risk Management investment and emerging trends?

<--- Score

36. What do we need to start doing?

<--- Score

37. What problems are you facing and how do you consider Third-Party Risk Management will circumvent those obstacles?

<--- Score

38. Are there Third-Party Risk Management problems defined?

<--- Score

39. What information do users need?

<--- Score

40. What tools and technologies are needed for a custom Third-Party Risk Management project?

<--- Score

41. Does our organization need more Third-Party Risk Management education?

<--- Score

42. Consider your own Third-Party Risk Management project. what types of organizational problems do you think might be causing or affecting your problem, based on the work done so far?

<--- Score

43. How do you assess your Third-Party Risk Management workforce capability and capacity needs, including skills, competencies, and staffing levels?

<--- Score

44. How does it fit into our organizational needs and tasks?

<--- Score

45. How do you identify the information basis for later specification of performance or acceptance criteria?

<--- Score

46. What are the expected benefits of Third-Party Risk Management to the business?
<--- Score

47. What prevents me from making the changes I know will make me a more effective Third-Party Risk Management leader?
<--- Score

48. Will a response program recognize when a crisis occurs and provide some level of response?
<--- Score

49. What vendors make products that address the Third-Party Risk Management needs?
<--- Score

50. Can Management personnel recognize the monetary benefit of Third-Party Risk Management?
<--- Score

Add up total points for this section:
_____ = Total points for this section

Divided by: _____ (number of statements answered) = _____
Average score for this section

Transfer your score to the Third-Party Risk Management Index at the beginning of the Self-Assessment.

CRITERION #2: DEFINE:

INTENT: Formulate the business problem. Define the problem, needs and objectives.

In my belief, the answer to this question is clearly defined:

5 Strongly Agree

4 Agree

3 Neutral

2 Disagree

1 Strongly Disagree

1. Is a fully trained team formed, supported, and committed to work on the Third-Party Risk Management improvements?
<--- Score

2. How was the 'as is' process map developed, reviewed, verified and validated?
<--- Score

3. Has a high-level 'as is' process map been completed, verified and validated?
<--- Score

4. Has the improvement team collected the 'voice of the customer' (obtained feedback – qualitative and quantitative)?
<--- Score

5. What would be the goal or target for a Third-Party Risk Management's improvement team?
<--- Score

6. What are the rough order estimates on cost savings/ opportunities that Third-Party Risk Management brings?
<--- Score

7. Does the team have regular meetings?
<--- Score

8. Is the team adequately staffed with the desired cross-functionality? If not, what additional resources are available to the team?
<--- Score

9. How and when will the baselines be defined?
<--- Score

10. Is the team equipped with available and reliable resources?
<--- Score

11. What are the compelling business reasons for embarking on Third-Party Risk Management?
<--- Score

12. How would you define the culture here?
<--- Score

13. What customer feedback methods were used to solicit their input?
<--- Score

14. Are audit criteria, scope, frequency and methods defined?
<--- Score

15. Are security/privacy roles and responsibilities formally defined?
<--- Score

16. Will team members perform Third-Party Risk Management work when assigned and in a timely fashion?
<--- Score

17. Do we all define Third-Party Risk Management in the same way?
<--- Score

18. What specifically is the problem? Where does it occur? When does it occur? What is its extent?
<--- Score

19. Are business processes mapped?
<--- Score

20. Is there regularly 100% attendance at the team meetings? If not, have appointed substitutes attended to preserve cross-functionality and full representation?

<--- Score

21. How do senior leaders promote an environment that fosters and requires legal and ethical behavior?
<--- Score

22. Are different versions of process maps needed to account for the different types of inputs?
<--- Score

23. What baselines are required to be defined and managed?
<--- Score

24. Is it clearly defined in and to your organization what you do?
<--- Score

25. Are improvement team members fully trained on Third-Party Risk Management?
<--- Score

26. What is the minimum educational requirement for potential new hires?
<--- Score

27. Is there a critical path to deliver Third-Party Risk Management results?
<--- Score

28. Is there a Third-Party Risk Management management charter, including business case, problem and goal statements, scope, milestones, roles and responsibilities, communication plan?
<--- Score

29. How can the value of Third-Party Risk Management be defined?
<--- Score

30. Is the team formed and are team leaders (Coaches and Management Leads) assigned?
<--- Score

31. Has/have the customer(s) been identified?
<--- Score

32. What defines Best in Class?
<--- Score

33. Is the current 'as is' process being followed? If not, what are the discrepancies?
<--- Score

34. How is the team tracking and documenting its work?
<--- Score

35. Are approval levels defined for contracts and supplements to contracts?
<--- Score

36. How often are the team meetings?
<--- Score

37. Who are the Third-Party Risk Management improvement team members, including Management Leads and Coaches?
<--- Score

38. Is data collected and displayed to better

understand customer(s) critical needs and requirements.
<--- Score

39. Has anyone else (internal or external to the organization) attempted to solve this problem or a similar one before? If so, what knowledge can be leveraged from these previous efforts?
<--- Score

40. How did the Third-Party Risk Management manager receive input to the development of a Third-Party Risk Management improvement plan and the estimated completion dates/times of each activity?
<--- Score

41. Is Third-Party Risk Management currently on schedule according to the plan?
<--- Score

42. Are roles and responsibilities formally defined?
<--- Score

43. What are the Roles and Responsibilities for each team member and its leadership? Where is this documented?
<--- Score

44. Has a team charter been developed and communicated?
<--- Score

45. Are team charters developed?
<--- Score

46. Who defines (or who defined) the rules and roles?

<--- Score

47. Are Required Metrics Defined?
<--- Score

48. What organizational structure is required?
<--- Score

49. Have specific policy objectives been defined?
<--- Score

50. In what way can we redefine the criteria of choice clients have in our category in our favor?
<--- Score

51. Is the team sponsored by a champion or business leader?
<--- Score

52. When is the estimated completion date?
<--- Score

53. When was the Third-Party Risk Management start date?
<--- Score

54. In what way can we redefine the criteria of choice in our category in our favor, as Method introduced style and design to cleaning and Virgin America returned glamor to flying?
<--- Score

55. What constraints exist that might impact the team?
<--- Score

56. Is the scope of Third-Party Risk Management defined?
<--- Score

57. Are customers identified and high impact areas defined?
<--- Score

58. What tools and roadmaps did you use for getting through the Define phase?
<--- Score

59. Have all of the relationships been defined properly?
<--- Score

60. Is there a completed SIPOC representation, describing the Suppliers, Inputs, Process, Outputs, and Customers?
<--- Score

61. How do you keep key subject matter experts in the loop?
<--- Score

62. Has the direction changed at all during the course of Third-Party Risk Management? If so, when did it change and why?
<--- Score

63. What are the dynamics of the communication plan?
<--- Score

64. If substitutes have been appointed, have they been briefed on the Third-Party Risk Management

goals and received regular communications as to the progress to date?
<--- Score

65. How would one define Third-Party Risk Management leadership?
<--- Score

66. Is the Third-Party Risk Management scope manageable?
<--- Score

67. Are customer(s) identified and segmented according to their different needs and requirements?
<--- Score

68. Have the customer needs been translated into specific, measurable requirements? How?
<--- Score

69. Are task requirements clearly defined?
<--- Score

70. How does the Third-Party Risk Management manager ensure against scope creep?
<--- Score

71. Have all basic functions of Third-Party Risk Management been defined?
<--- Score

72. How will the Third-Party Risk Management team and the organization measure complete success of Third-Party Risk Management?
<--- Score

73. Has everyone on the team, including the team leaders, been properly trained?
<--- Score

74. Are there any constraints known that bear on the ability to perform Third-Party Risk Management work? How is the team addressing them?
<--- Score

75. When are meeting minutes sent out? Who is on the distribution list?
<--- Score

76. Is Third-Party Risk Management linked to key business goals and objectives?
<--- Score

77. How will variation in the actual durations of each activity be dealt with to ensure that the expected Third-Party Risk Management results are met?
<--- Score

78. What key business process output measure(s) does Third-Party Risk Management leverage and how?
<--- Score

79. Are accountability and ownership for Third-Party Risk Management clearly defined?
<--- Score

80. Is Third-Party Risk Management Required?
<--- Score

81. Has the Third-Party Risk Management work been fairly and/or equitably divided and delegated among team members who are qualified and capable to

perform the work? Has everyone contributed?
<--- Score

82. Are there different segments of customers?
<--- Score

83. Is there a completed, verified, and validated high-level 'as is' (not 'should be' or 'could be') business process map?
<--- Score

84. Do the problem and goal statements meet the SMART criteria (specific, measurable, attainable, relevant, and time-bound)?
<--- Score

85. What critical content must be communicated – who, what, when, where, and how?
<--- Score

86. Is full participation by members in regularly held team meetings guaranteed?
<--- Score

87. Has a project plan, Gantt chart, or similar been developed/completed?
<--- Score

88. Will team members regularly document their Third-Party Risk Management work?
<--- Score

89. Is the improvement team aware of the different versions of a process: what they think it is vs. what it actually is vs. what it should be vs. what it could be?
<--- Score

90. What are the boundaries of the scope? What is in bounds and what is not? What is the start point? What is the stop point?
<--- Score

Add up total points for this section:
_ _ _ _ _ = Total points for this section

Divided by: _ _ _ _ _ _ (number of statements answered) = _ _ _ _ _ _
Average score for this section

Transfer your score to the Third-Party Risk Management Index at the beginning of the Self-Assessment.

CRITERION #3: MEASURE:

INTENT: Gather the correct data. Measure the current performance and evolution of the situation.

In my belief, the answer to this question is clearly defined:

5 Strongly Agree

4 Agree

3 Neutral

2 Disagree

1 Strongly Disagree

1. What are the agreed upon definitions of the high impact areas, defect(s), unit(s), and opportunities that will figure into the process capability metrics?
<--- Score

2. **What methods are feasible and acceptable to estimate the impact of reforms?**
<--- Score

3. How to measure variability?
<--- Score

4. How frequently do you track Third-Party Risk Management measures?
<--- Score

5. Have the types of risks that may impact Third-Party Risk Management been identified and analyzed?
<--- Score

6. What are my customers expectations and measures?
<--- Score

7. What should be measured?
<--- Score

8. Why do measure/indicators matter?
<--- Score

9. Are you taking your company in the direction of better and revenue or cheaper and cost?
<--- Score

10. What particular quality tools did the team find helpful in establishing measurements?
<--- Score

11. Who participated in the data collection for measurements?
<--- Score

12. Do staff have the necessary skills to collect, analyze, and report data?
<--- Score

13. Can we do Third-Party Risk Management without complex (expensive) analysis?

<--- Score

14. Which customers cant participate in our Third-Party Risk Management domain because they lack skills, wealth, or convenient access to existing solutions?

<--- Score

15. How will your organization measure success?

<--- Score

16. How large is the gap between current performance and the customer-specified (goal) performance?

<--- Score

17. Among the Third-Party Risk Management product and service cost to be estimated, which is considered hardest to estimate?

<--- Score

18. How do we do risk analysis of rare, cascading, catastrophic events?

<--- Score

19. Are the measurements objective?

<--- Score

20. Can We Measure the Return on Analysis?

<--- Score

21. Does the Third-Party Risk Management task fit the client's priorities?

<--- Score

22. What is the right balance of time and resources between investigation, analysis, and discussion and dissemination?
<--- Score

23. Are there measurements based on task performance?
<--- Score

24. Is there a Performance Baseline?
<--- Score

25. Which customers can't participate in our market because they lack skills, wealth, or convenient access to existing solutions?
<--- Score

26. What are our key indicators that you will measure, analyze and track?
<--- Score

27. Have all non-recommended alternatives been analyzed in sufficient detail?
<--- Score

28. Is a solid data collection plan established that includes measurement systems analysis?
<--- Score

29. How will success or failure be measured?
<--- Score

30. What about Third-Party Risk Management Analysis of results?

<--- Score

31. How do you identify and analyze stakeholders and their interests?
<--- Score

32. Have the concerns of stakeholders to help identify and define potential barriers been obtained and analyzed?
<--- Score

33. Meeting the challenge: are missed Third-Party Risk Management opportunities costing us money?
<--- Score

34. Do we effectively measure and reward individual and team performance?
<--- Score

35. Have changes been properly/adequately analyzed for effect?
<--- Score

36. Was a data collection plan established?
<--- Score

37. How can we measure the performance?
<--- Score

38. Do we aggressively reward and promote the people who have the biggest impact on creating excellent Third-Party Risk Management services/ products?
<--- Score

39. What charts has the team used to display the components of variation in the process?
<--- Score

40. What are the types and number of measures to use?
<--- Score

41. Are priorities and opportunities deployed to your suppliers, partners, and collaborators to ensure organizational alignment?
<--- Score

42. What measurements are being captured?
<--- Score

43. How will effects be measured?
<--- Score

44. How will measures be used to manage and adapt?
<--- Score

45. What evidence is there and what is measured?
<--- Score

46. What key measures identified indicate the performance of the business process?
<--- Score

47. Is it possible to estimate the impact of unanticipated complexity such as wrong or failed assumptions, feedback, etc. on proposed reforms?
<--- Score

48. How frequently do we track measures?
<--- Score

49. What are the key input variables? What are the key process variables? What are the key output variables?
<--- Score

50. Which Stakeholder Characteristics Are Analyzed?
<--- Score

51. Is Process Variation Displayed/Communicated?
<--- Score

52. How Will We Measure Success?
<--- Score

53. Does the practice systematically track and analyze outcomes related for accountability and quality improvement?
<--- Score

54. What will be measured?
<--- Score

55. How do we focus on what is right -not who is right?
<--- Score

56. Are we taking our company in the direction of better and revenue or cheaper and cost?
<--- Score

57. Is this an issue for analysis or intuition?
<--- Score

58. What is measured?
<--- Score

59. Customer Measures: How Do Customers See Us?
<--- Score

60. What are the costs of reform?
<--- Score

61. Are key measures identified and agreed upon?
<--- Score

62. Is long term and short term variability accounted for?
<--- Score

63. What is an unallowable cost?
<--- Score

64. What is the total cost related to deploying Third-Party Risk Management, including any consulting or professional services?
<--- Score

65. Why do the measurements/indicators matter?
<--- Score

66. Why should we expend time and effort to implement measurement?
<--- Score

67. How is progress measured?
<--- Score

68. Where is it measured?
<--- Score

69. Is key measure data collection planned and executed, process variation displayed and

communicated and performance baselined?
<--- Score

70. Have you found any 'ground fruit' or 'low-hanging fruit' for immediate remedies to the gap in performance?
<--- Score

71. What Relevant Entities could be measured?
<--- Score

72. How are you going to measure success?
<--- Score

73. What potential environmental factors impact the Third-Party Risk Management effort?
<--- Score

74. Are process variation components displayed/communicated using suitable charts, graphs, plots?
<--- Score

75. Are high impact defects defined and identified in the business process?
<--- Score

76. What are the uncertainties surrounding estimates of impact?
<--- Score

77. Is performance measured?
<--- Score

78. Does Third-Party Risk Management systematically track and analyze outcomes for accountability and quality improvement?

<--- Score

79. What data was collected (past, present, future/ongoing)?
<--- Score

80. Who should receive measurement reports ?
<--- Score

81. Is data collected on key measures that were identified?
<--- Score

82. Why Measure?
<--- Score

83. How is Knowledge Management Measured?
<--- Score

84. Are the units of measure consistent?
<--- Score

85. How do you measure success?
<--- Score

86. What to measure and why?
<--- Score

87. What has the team done to assure the stability and accuracy of the measurement process?
<--- Score

88. Is the solution cost-effective?
<--- Score

89. What are your key Third-Party Risk

Management organizational performance measures, including key short and longer-term financial measures?

<--- Score

90. How are measurements made?
<--- Score

91. Which methods and measures do you use to determine workforce engagement and workforce satisfaction?

<--- Score

92. When is Knowledge Management Measured?
<--- Score

93. How do senior leaders create a focus on action to accomplish the organization s objectives and improve performance?

<--- Score

94. Is data collection planned and executed?
<--- Score

95. How is the value delivered by Third-Party Risk Management being measured?
<--- Score

96. Will We Aggregate Measures across Priorities?
<--- Score

97. Does Third-Party Risk Management analysis show the relationships among important Third-Party Risk Management factors?

<--- Score

98. Why identify and analyze stakeholders and their interests?

<--- Score

99. Are losses documented, analyzed, and remedial processes developed to prevent future losses?

<--- Score

100. What measurements are possible, practicable and meaningful?

<--- Score

101. How to measure lifecycle phases?

<--- Score

102. Are there any easy-to-implement alternatives to Third-Party Risk Management? Sometimes other solutions are available that do not require the cost implications of a full-blown project?

<--- Score

103. How will you measure your Third-Party Risk Management effectiveness?

<--- Score

104. Does Third-Party Risk Management analysis isolate the fundamental causes of problems?

<--- Score

105. How can you measure Third-Party Risk Management in a systematic way?

<--- Score

106. What are measures?

<--- Score

Add up total points for this section:
_____ = Total points for this section

Divided by: _____ (number of
statements answered) = _____
Average score for this section

Transfer your score to the Third-Party
Risk Management Index at the beginning
of the Self-Assessment.

CRITERION #4: ANALYZE:

INTENT: Analyze causes, assumptions and hypotheses.

In my belief, the answer to this question is clearly defined:

5 Strongly Agree

4 Agree

3 Neutral

2 Disagree

1 Strongly Disagree

1. What conclusions were drawn from the team's data collection and analysis? How did the team reach these conclusions?
<--- Score

2. What were the crucial 'moments of truth' on the process map?
<--- Score

3. How do we promote understanding that

opportunity for improvement is not criticism of the status quo, or the people who created the status quo?

<--- Score

4. What process should we select for improvement?

<--- Score

5. Is Data and process analysis, root cause analysis and quantifying the gap/opportunity in place?

<--- Score

6. Do you, as a leader, bounce back quickly from setbacks?

<--- Score

7. How do mission and objectives affect the Third-Party Risk Management processes of our organization?

<--- Score

8. How was the detailed process map generated, verified, and validated?

<--- Score

9. What other organizational variables, such as reward systems or communication systems, affect the performance of this Third-Party Risk Management process?

<--- Score

10. What are your current levels and trends in key measures or indicators of Third-Party Risk Management product and process performance that are important to and directly serve your customers? how do these results compare with

**the performance of your competitors and other
organizations with similar offerings?**
<--- Score

11. Have any additional benefits been identified that
will result from closing all or most of the gaps?
<--- Score

12. Were any designed experiments used to generate
additional insight into the data analysis?
<--- Score

13. Was a detailed process map created to amplify
critical steps of the 'as is' business process?
<--- Score

14. Did any value-added analysis or 'lean thinking'
take place to identify some of the gaps shown on the
'as is' process map?
<--- Score

15. What are our Third-Party Risk Management
Processes?
<--- Score

16. What tools were used to narrow the list of possible
causes?
<--- Score

17. Is the Third-Party Risk Management process
severely broken such that a re-design is necessary?
<--- Score

18. How does the organization define, manage, and
improve its Third-Party Risk Management processes?
<--- Score

19. Do our leaders quickly bounce back from setbacks?

<--- Score

20. What tools were used to generate the list of possible causes?

<--- Score

21. How often will data be collected for measures?

<--- Score

22. Can we add value to the current Third-Party Risk Management decision-making process (largely qualitative) by incorporating uncertainty modeling (more quantitative)?

<--- Score

23. Were there any improvement opportunities identified from the process analysis?

<--- Score

24. How do you use Third-Party Risk Management data and information to support organizational decision making and innovation?

<--- Score

25. What did the team gain from developing a sub-process map?

<--- Score

26. Think about the functions involved in your Third-Party Risk Management project. what processes flow from these functions?

<--- Score

27. How is the way you as the leader think and process information affecting your organizational culture?
<--- Score

28. Was a cause-and-effect diagram used to explore the different types of causes (or sources of variation)?
<--- Score

29. What controls do we have in place to protect data?
<--- Score

30. Are gaps between current performance and the goal performance identified?
<--- Score

31. What were the financial benefits resulting from any 'ground fruit or low-hanging fruit' (quick fixes)?
<--- Score

32. Identify an operational issue in your organization. for example, could a particular task be done more quickly or more efficiently?
<--- Score

33. What other jobs or tasks affect the performance of the steps in the Third-Party Risk Management process?
<--- Score

34. How do you measure the Operational performance of your key work systems and processes, including productivity, cycle time, and other appropriate measures of process effectiveness, efficiency, and innovation?
<--- Score

35. Have the problem and goal statements been updated to reflect the additional knowledge gained from the analyze phase?
<--- Score

36. What quality tools were used to get through the analyze phase?
<--- Score

37. Is the suppliers process defined and controlled?
<--- Score

38. An organizationally feasible system request is one that considers the mission, goals and objectives of the organization. key questions are: is the solution request practical and will it solve a problem or take advantage of an opportunity to achieve company goals?
<--- Score

39. What are your current levels and trends in key Third-Party Risk Management measures or indicators of product and process performance that are important to and directly serve your customers?
<--- Score

40. Record-keeping requirements flow from the records needed as inputs, outputs, controls and for transformation of a Third-Party Risk Management process. ask yourself: are the records needed as inputs to the Third-Party Risk Management process available?
<--- Score

41. What are the revised rough estimates of the financial savings/opportunity for Third-Party Risk Management improvements?
<--- Score

42. Do your employees have the opportunity to do what they do best everyday?
<--- Score

43. What are the best opportunities for value improvement?
<--- Score

44. Where is the data coming from to measure compliance?
<--- Score

45. Think about some of the processes you undertake within your organization. which do you own?
<--- Score

46. A compounding model resolution with available relevant data can often provide insight towards a solution methodology; which Third-Party Risk Management models, tools and techniques are necessary?
<--- Score

47. What are the disruptive Third-Party Risk Management technologies that enable our organization to radically change our business processes?
<--- Score

48. When conducting a business process

reengineering study, what should we look for when trying to identify business processes to change?
<--- Score

49. What is the cost of poor quality as supported by the team's analysis?
<--- Score

50. Is the performance gap determined?
<--- Score

51. Were Pareto charts (or similar) used to portray the 'heavy hitters' (or key sources of variation)?
<--- Score

52. Is the gap/opportunity displayed and communicated in financial terms?
<--- Score

53. Did any additional data need to be collected?
<--- Score

54. What does the data say about the performance of the business process?
<--- Score

55. What successful thing are we doing today that may be blinding us to new growth opportunities?
<--- Score

Add up total points for this section:
_ _ _ _ _ = Total points for this section

Divided by: _ _ _ _ _ _ (number of statements answered) = _ _ _ _ _ _

Average score for this section

Transfer your score to the Third-Party
Risk Management Index at the beginning
of the Self-Assessment.

CRITERION #5: IMPROVE:

INTENT: Develop a practical solution. Innovate, establish and test the solution and to measure the results.

In my belief, the answer to this question is clearly defined:

5 Strongly Agree

4 Agree

3 Neutral

2 Disagree

1 Strongly Disagree

1. How do we keep improving Third-Party Risk Management?
<--- Score

2. Who will be using the results of the measurement activities?
<--- Score

3. What is the risk?

<--- Score

4. How will you measure the results?
<--- Score

5. Who will be responsible for documenting the Third-Party Risk Management requirements in detail?
<--- Score

6. What is the team's contingency plan for potential problems occurring in implementation?
<--- Score

7. How do you improve workforce health, safety, and security? What are your performance measures and improvement goals for each of these workforce needs and what are any significant differences in these factors and performance measures or targets for different workplace environments?
<--- Score

8. What actually has to improve and by how much?
<--- Score

9. Is there a high likelihood that any recommendations will achieve their intended results?
<--- Score

10. What does the 'should be' process map/design look like?
<--- Score

11. What tools were used to evaluate the potential solutions?

<--- Score

12. What do we want to improve?
<--- Score

13. Who will be responsible for making the decisions to include or exclude requested changes once Third-Party Risk Management is underway?
<--- Score

14. To what extent does management recognize Third-Party Risk Management as a tool to increase the results?
<--- Score

15. How do we Improve Third-Party Risk Management service perception, and satisfaction?
<--- Score

16. How important is the completion of a recognized college or graduate-level degree program in the hiring decision?
<--- Score

17. How can we improve performance?
<--- Score

18. How can we improve Third-Party Risk Management?
<--- Score

19. Are we Assessing Third-Party Risk Management and Risk?
<--- Score

20. Were any criteria developed to assist the team in

testing and evaluating potential solutions?
<--- Score

21. What tools were used to tap into the creativity and encourage 'outside the box' thinking?
<--- Score

22. Is there a cost/benefit analysis of optimal solution(s)?
<--- Score

23. What needs improvement?
<--- Score

24. How will we know that a change is improvement?
<--- Score

25. Do we cover the five essential competencies-Communication, Collaboration,Innovation, Adaptability, and Leadership that improve an organization's ability to leverage the new Third-Party Risk Management in a volatile global economy?
<--- Score

26. What error proofing will be done to address some of the discrepancies observed in the 'as is' process?
<--- Score

27. How will you know when its improved?
<--- Score

28. Are there any constraints (technical, political, cultural, or otherwise) that would inhibit certain solutions?
<--- Score

29. How do you improve your likelihood of success ?
<--- Score

30. Are improved process ('should be') maps modified based on pilot data and analysis?
<--- Score

31. How can skill-level changes improve Third-Party Risk Management?
<--- Score

32. Is the solution technically practical?
<--- Score

33. Are new and improved process ('should be') maps developed?
<--- Score

34. How will the team or the process owner(s) monitor the implementation plan to see that it is working as intended?
<--- Score

35. How do you use other indicators, such as workforce retention, absenteeism, grievances, safety, and productivity, to assess and improve workforce engagement?
<--- Score

36. How do we improve productivity?
<--- Score

37. Is Supporting Third-Party Risk Management documentation required?
<--- Score

38. Is a contingency plan established?
<--- Score

39. Is the implementation plan designed?
<--- Score

40. Why improve in the first place?
<--- Score

41. How will the organization know that the solution worked?
<--- Score

42. Describe the design of the pilot and what tests were conducted, if any?
<--- Score

43. How significant is the improvement in the eyes of the end user?
<--- Score

44. What is Third-Party Risk Management's impact on utilizing the best solution(s)?
<--- Score

45. At what point will vulnerability assessments be performed once Third-Party Risk Management is put into production (e.g., ongoing Risk Management after implementation)?
<--- Score

46. How do the Third-Party Risk Management results compare with the performance of your competitors and other organizations with similar offerings?
<--- Score

47. Was a pilot designed for the proposed solution(s)?
<--- Score

48. Are the best solutions selected?
<--- Score

49. What communications are necessary to support the implementation of the solution?
<--- Score

50. How will you know that you have improved?
<--- Score

51. What lessons, if any, from a pilot were incorporated into the design of the full-scale solution?
<--- Score

52. Is pilot data collected and analyzed?
<--- Score

53. How did the team generate the list of possible solutions?
<--- Score

54. In the past few months, what is the smallest change we have made that has had the biggest positive result? What was it about that small change that produced the large return?
<--- Score

55. What are the implications of this decision 10 minutes, 10 months, and 10 years from now?
<--- Score

56. How do we measure risk?

<--- Score

57. What to do with the results or outcomes of measurements?
<--- Score

58. What should a proof of concept or pilot accomplish?
<--- Score

59. For decision problems, how do you develop a decision statement?
<--- Score

60. What improvements have been achieved?
<--- Score

61. How do we go about Comparing Third-Party Risk Management approaches/solutions?
<--- Score

62. What can we do to improve?
<--- Score

63. How to Improve?
<--- Score

64. What resources are required for the improvement effort?
<--- Score

65. What went well, what should change, what can improve?
<--- Score

66. What were the underlying assumptions on the

cost-benefit analysis?
<--- Score

67. Can the solution be designed and implemented within an acceptable time period?
<--- Score

68. Is a solution implementation plan established, including schedule/work breakdown structure, resources, risk management plan, cost/budget, and control plan?
<--- Score

69. How does the solution remove the key sources of issues discovered in the analyze phase?
<--- Score

70. Who controls key decisions that will be made?
<--- Score

71. How Do We Link Measurement and Risk?
<--- Score

72. What attendant changes will need to be made to ensure that the solution is successful?
<--- Score

73. What is the implementation plan?
<--- Score

74. Risk factors: what are the characteristics of Third-Party Risk Management that make it risky?
<--- Score

75. Who controls the risk?
<--- Score

76. What is the magnitude of the improvements?
<--- Score

77. What evaluation strategy is needed and what needs to be done to assure its implementation and use?
<--- Score

78. Is there a small-scale pilot for proposed improvement(s)? What conclusions were drawn from the outcomes of a pilot?
<--- Score

79. For estimation problems, how do you develop an estimation statement?
<--- Score

80. Does the goal represent a desired result that can be measured?
<--- Score

81. How do you measure progress and evaluate training effectiveness?
<--- Score

82. How do we measure improved Third-Party Risk Management service perception, and satisfaction?
<--- Score

83. Is the optimal solution selected based on testing and analysis?
<--- Score

84. Who are the people involved in developing and implementing Third-Party Risk Management?

<--- Score

85. How do we decide how much to remunerate an employee?

<--- Score

86. What tools were most useful during the improve phase?

<--- Score

87. Do we get business results?

<--- Score

88. Risk events: what are the things that could go wrong?

<--- Score

89. Are possible solutions generated and tested?

<--- Score

90. Is the measure understandable to a variety of people?

<--- Score

91. If you could go back in time five years, what decision would you make differently? What is your best guess as to what decision you're making today you might regret five years from now?

<--- Score

92. How does the team improve its work?

<--- Score

Add up total points for this section:
_ _ _ _ _ = Total points for this section

Divided by: _____ (number of
statements answered) = _____
Average score for this section

Transfer your score to the Third-Party
Risk Management Index at the beginning
of the Self-Assessment.

CRITERION #6: CONTROL:

INTENT: Implement the practical solution. Maintain the performance and correct possible complications.

In my belief, the answer to this question is clearly defined:

5 Strongly Agree

4 Agree

3 Neutral

2 Disagree

1 Strongly Disagree

1. Is reporting being used or needed?
<--- Score

2. Does the response plan contain a definite closed loop continual improvement scheme (e.g., plan-do-check-act)?
<--- Score

3. Do you monitor the effectiveness of your Third-

Party Risk Management activities?

<--- Score

4. Are pertinent alerts monitored, analyzed and distributed to appropriate personnel?

<--- Score

5. How do controls support value?

<--- Score

6. Were the planned controls in place?

<--- Score

7. What quality tools were useful in the control phase?

<--- Score

8. Is a response plan established and deployed?

<--- Score

9. What are the key elements of your Third-Party Risk Management performance improvement system, including your evaluation, organizational learning, and innovation processes?

<--- Score

10. Why is change control necessary?

<--- Score

11. What is your quality control system?

<--- Score

12. What can you control?

<--- Score

13. Who controls critical resources?

<--- Score

14. What key inputs and outputs are being measured on an ongoing basis?

<--- Score

15. Is there a standardized process?

<--- Score

16. What do we stand for--and what are we against?

<--- Score

17. What are we attempting to measure/monitor?

<--- Score

18. How might the organization capture best practices and lessons learned so as to leverage improvements across the business?

<--- Score

19. How will report readings be checked to effectively monitor performance?

<--- Score

20. What are the known security controls?

<--- Score

21. Who is the Third-Party Risk Management process owner?

<--- Score

22. Are documented procedures clear and easy to follow for the operators?

<--- Score

23. Has the improved process and its steps been

standardized?

<--- Score

24. What other systems, operations, processes, and infrastructures (hiring practices, staffing, training, incentives/rewards, metrics/dashboards/scorecards, etc.) need updates, additions, changes, or deletions in order to facilitate knowledge transfer and improvements?

<--- Score

25. How does your workforce performance management system support high-performance work and workforce engagement; consider workforce compensation, reward, recognition, and incentive practices; and reinforce a customer and business focus and achievement of your action plans?

<--- Score

26. How will the process owner and team be able to hold the gains?

<--- Score

27. Whats the best design framework for Third-Party Risk Management organization now that, in a post industrial-age if the top-down, command and control model is no longer relevant?

<--- Score

28. Are suggested corrective/restorative actions indicated on the response plan for known causes to problems that might surface?

<--- Score

29. How can we best use all of our knowledge

repositories to enhance learning and sharing?
<--- Score

30. Is there documentation that will support the successful operation of the improvement?
<--- Score

31. Is new knowledge gained imbedded in the response plan?
<--- Score

32. What should we measure to verify efficiency gains?
<--- Score

33. Does job training on the documented procedures need to be part of the process team's education and training?
<--- Score

34. Do we monitor the Third-Party Risk Management decisions made and fine tune them as they evolve?
<--- Score

35. Do the Third-Party Risk Management decisions we make today help people and the planet tomorrow?
<--- Score

36. Who will be in control?
<--- Score

37. Implementation Planning- is a pilot needed to test the changes before a full roll out occurs?
<--- Score

38. Does a troubleshooting guide exist or is it needed?
<--- Score

39. Is there a Third-Party Risk Management Communication plan covering who needs to get what information when?
<--- Score

40. Will existing staff require re-training, for example, to learn new business processes?
<--- Score

41. Have new or revised work instructions resulted?
<--- Score

42. How do our controls stack up?
<--- Score

43. In the case of a Third-Party Risk Management project, the criteria for the audit derive from implementation objectives. an audit of a Third-Party Risk Management project involves assessing whether the recommendations outlined for implementation have been met. in other words, can we track that any Third-Party Risk Management project is implemented as planned, and is it working?
<--- Score

44. If there currently is no plan, will a plan be developed?
<--- Score

45. Will any special training be provided for results interpretation?

<--- Score

46. Is there a recommended audit plan for routine surveillance inspections of Third-Party Risk Management's gains?
<--- Score

47. What should the next improvement project be that is related to Third-Party Risk Management?
<--- Score

48. What should we measure to verify effectiveness gains?
<--- Score

49. Were the planned controls working?
<--- Score

50. What is our theory of human motivation, and how does our compensation plan fit with that view?
<--- Score

51. Do the decisions we make today help people and the planet tomorrow?
<--- Score

52. What other areas of the organization might benefit from the Third-Party Risk Management team's improvements, knowledge, and learning?
<--- Score

53. Does the Third-Party Risk Management performance meet the customer's requirements?
<--- Score

54. Is there a transfer of ownership and knowledge to process owner and process team tasked with the responsibilities.
<--- Score

55. Against what alternative is success being measured?
<--- Score

56. Are there documented procedures?
<--- Score

57. Is knowledge gained on process shared and institutionalized?
<--- Score

58. Who has control over resources?
<--- Score

59. How likely is the current Third-Party Risk Management plan to come in on schedule or on budget?
<--- Score

60. What are the critical parameters to watch?
<--- Score

61. Is a response plan in place for when the input, process, or output measures indicate an 'out-of-control' condition?
<--- Score

62. How do you encourage people to take control and responsibility?
<--- Score

63. Are new process steps, standards, and documentation ingrained into normal operations?
<--- Score

64. What is the recommended frequency of auditing?
<--- Score

65. How will new or emerging customer needs/requirements be checked/communicated to orient the process toward meeting the new specifications and continually reducing variation?
<--- Score

66. What is your theory of human motivation, and how does your compensation plan fit with that view?
<--- Score

67. Are operating procedures consistent?
<--- Score

68. What is the control/monitoring plan?
<--- Score

69. What are your results for key measures or indicators of the accomplishment of your Third-Party Risk Management strategy and action plans, including building and strengthening core competencies?
<--- Score

70. How will input, process, and output variables be checked to detect for sub-optimal conditions?
<--- Score

71. Are controls in place and consistently applied?
<--- Score

72. How will the process owner verify improvement in present and future sigma levels, process capabilities?
<--- Score

73. How will the day-to-day responsibilities for monitoring and continual improvement be transferred from the improvement team to the process owner?
<--- Score

74. Is there a control plan in place for sustaining improvements (short and long-term)?
<--- Score

75. Where do ideas that reach policy makers and planners as proposals for Third-Party Risk Management strengthening and reform actually originate?
<--- Score

76. Is there a documented and implemented monitoring plan?
<--- Score

77. How do we enable market innovation while controlling security and privacy?
<--- Score

78. Does Third-Party Risk Management appropriately measure and monitor risk?
<--- Score

Add up total points for this section:
_____ = Total points for this section

Divided by: _____ (number of
statements answered) = _____
Average score for this section

Transfer your score to the Third-Party
Risk Management Index at the beginning
of the Self-Assessment.

CRITERION #7: SUSTAIN:

INTENT: Retain the benefits.

In my belief, the answer to this question is clearly defined:

5 Strongly Agree

4 Agree

3 Neutral

2 Disagree

1 Strongly Disagree

1. Would you rather sell to knowledgeable and informed customers or to uninformed customers?
<--- Score

2. What is our formula for success in Third-Party Risk Management ?
<--- Score

3. Is there a lack of internal resources to do this work?
<--- Score

4. What would I recommend my friend do if he were facing this dilemma?

<--- Score

5. Who Uses What?

<--- Score

6. Why should we adopt a Third-Party Risk Management framework?

<--- Score

7. Have new benefits been realized?

<--- Score

8. If our company went out of business tomorrow, would anyone who doesn't get a paycheck here care?

<--- Score

9. How would our PR, marketing, and social media change if we did not use outside agencies?

<--- Score

10. In the past year, what have you done (or could you have done) to increase the accurate perception of this company/brand as ethical and honest?

<--- Score

11. Is a Third-Party Risk Management Team Work effort in place?

<--- Score

12. What trouble can we get into?

<--- Score

13. What is the range of capabilities?

<--- Score

14. How long will it take to change?
<--- Score

15. Is there any reason to believe the opposite of my current belief?
<--- Score

16. If we weren't already in this business, would we enter it today? And if not, what are we going to do about it?
<--- Score

17. What principles do we value?
<--- Score

18. Which criteria are used to determine which projects are going to be pursued or discarded?
<--- Score

19. Are assumptions made in Third-Party Risk Management stated explicitly?
<--- Score

20. How will we ensure we get what we expected?
<--- Score

21. Where is our petri dish?
<--- Score

22. What is something you believe that nearly no one agrees with you on?
<--- Score

23. What are the success criteria that will indicate that

Third-Party Risk Management objectives have been met and the benefits delivered?
<--- Score

24. How do I stay inspired?
<--- Score

25. What do we do when new problems arise?
<--- Score

26. How is business? Why?
<--- Score

27. Which functions and people interact with the supplier and or customer?
<--- Score

28. What is Tricky About This?
<--- Score

29. Were lessons learned captured and communicated?
<--- Score

30. What is our competitive advantage?
<--- Score

31. How do we keep the momentum going?
<--- Score

32. What is performance excellence?
<--- Score

33. What are our long-range and short-range goals?
<--- Score

34. What will be the consequences to the stakeholder (financial, reputation etc) if Third-Party Risk Management does not go ahead or fails to deliver the objectives?
<--- Score

35. What kind of crime could a potential new hire have committed that would not only not disqualify him/her from being hired by our organization, but would actually indicate that he/she might be a particularly good fit?
<--- Score

36. How do we Lead with Third-Party Risk Management in Mind?
<--- Score

37. Are we relevant? Will we be relevant five years from now? Ten?
<--- Score

38. Do you see more potential in people than they do in themselves?
<--- Score

39. What is our question?
<--- Score

40. Who will manage the integration of tools?
<--- Score

41. Is the Third-Party Risk Management organization completing tasks effectively and efficiently?
<--- Score

42. How can you negotiate Third-Party Risk Management successfully with a stubborn boss, an irate client, or a deceitful coworker?
<--- Score

43. Why are Third-Party Risk Management skills important?
<--- Score

44. If you had to rebuild your organization without any traditional competitive advantages (i.e., no killer a technology, promising research, innovative product/service delivery model, etc.), how would your people have to approach their work and collaborate together in order to create the necessary conditions for success?
<--- Score

45. What are the gaps in my knowledge and experience?
<--- Score

46. Is our strategy driving our strategy? Or is the way in which we allocate resources driving our strategy?
<--- Score

47. Who do we think the world wants us to be?
<--- Score

48. What happens at this company when people fail?
<--- Score

49. Do you have an implicit bias for capital investments over people investments?
<--- Score

50. What are the rules and assumptions my industry operates under? What if the opposite were true?
<--- Score

51. Who will use it?
<--- Score

52. Who is responsible for errors?
<--- Score

53. Schedule -can it be done in the given time?
<--- Score

54. What are the usability implications of Third-Party Risk Management actions?
<--- Score

55. What happens if you do not have enough funding?
<--- Score

56. Who do we want our customers to become?
<--- Score

57. Are the assumptions believable and achievable?
<--- Score

58. How likely is it that a customer would recommend our company to a friend or colleague?
<--- Score

59. What happens when a new employee joins the organization?
<--- Score

60. What knowledge, skills and characteristics mark a good Third-Party Risk Management project manager?

<--- Score

61. How to Secure Third-Party Risk Management?

<--- Score

62. Legal and contractual - are we allowed to do this?

<--- Score

63. If you were responsible for initiating and implementing major changes in your organization, what steps might you take to ensure acceptance of those changes?

<--- Score

64. What is the purpose of Third-Party Risk Management in relation to the mission?

<--- Score

65. Do you have any supplemental information to add to this checklist?

<--- Score

66. How do we foster innovation?

<--- Score

67. Is the impact that Third-Party Risk Management has shown?

<--- Score

68. You may have created your customer policies at a time when you lacked resources, technology

wasn't up-to-snuff, or low service levels were the industry norm. Have those circumstances changed?

<--- Score

69. Are we changing as fast as the world around us?
<--- Score

70. What is it like to work for me?
<--- Score

71. How do we provide a safe environment -physically and emotionally?

<--- Score

72. Who is responsible for ensuring appropriate resources (time, people and money) are allocated to Third-Party Risk Management?
<--- Score

73. What is the overall business strategy?

<--- Score

74. Who are you going to put out of business, and why?
<--- Score

75. Are you satisfied with your current role? If not, what is missing from it?
<--- Score

76. Who sets the Third-Party Risk Management standards?

<--- Score

77. What are the critical success factors?

<--- Score

78. Who else should we help?
<--- Score

79. Will it be accepted by users?
<--- Score

80. In what ways are Third-Party Risk Management vendors and us interacting to ensure safe and effective use?
<--- Score

81. Do we have the right capabilities and capacities?
<--- Score

82. Are we / should we be Revolutionary or evolutionary?
<--- Score

83. Can we maintain our growth without detracting from the factors that have contributed to our success?
<--- Score

84. Will I get fired?
<--- Score

85. What is our Third-Party Risk Management Strategy?
<--- Score

86. What are internal and external Third-Party Risk Management relations?
<--- Score

87. How will you know that the Third-Party Risk Management project has been successful?
<--- Score

88. How Do We Know if We Are Successful?
<--- Score

89. Are new benefits received and understood?
<--- Score

90. Have highly satisfied employees?
<--- Score

91. What is the estimated value of the project?
<--- Score

92. But does it really, really work?
<--- Score

93. What business benefits will Third-Party Risk Management goals deliver if achieved?
<--- Score

94. Have benefits been optimized with all key stakeholders?
<--- Score

95. Who is going to care?
<--- Score

96. Think of your Third-Party Risk Management project. what are the main functions?
<--- Score

97. How do we go about Securing Third-Party Risk

Management?

<--- Score

98. How do we accomplish our long range Third-Party Risk Management goals?

<--- Score

99. If we do not follow, then how to lead?

<--- Score

100. What are we challenging, in the sense that Mac challenged the PC or Dove tackled the Beauty Myth?

<--- Score

101. How can we become more high-tech but still be high touch?

<--- Score

102. Do Third-Party Risk Management rules make a reasonable demand on a users capabilities?

<--- Score

103. Are we making progress?

<--- Score

104. What are the long-term Third-Party Risk Management goals?

<--- Score

105. What is the mission of the organization?

<--- Score

106. Are there Third-Party Risk Management Models?

<--- Score

107. What am I trying to prove to myself, and how

might it be hijacking my life and business success?
<--- Score

108. Among our stronger employees, how many
see themselves at the company in three years? How
many would leave for a 10 percent raise from another
company?
<--- Score

109. Who is the main stakeholder, with ultimate
responsibility for driving Third-Party Risk
Management forward?
<--- Score

**110. How will we insure seamless interoperability
of Third-Party Risk Management moving forward?**
<--- Score

111. Will there be any necessary staff changes
(redundancies or new hires)?
<--- Score

112. Do I know what I'm doing? And who do I call if I
don't?
<--- Score

113. Have totally satisfied customers?
<--- Score

114. How does Third-Party Risk Management
integrate with other business initiatives?
<--- Score

115. Who are our customers?
<--- Score

116. How do we ensure that implementations of Third-Party Risk Management products are done in a way that ensures safety?

<--- Score

117. What will drive Third-Party Risk Management change?

<--- Score

118. How can we incorporate support to ensure safe and effective use of Third-Party Risk Management into the services that we provide?

<--- Score

119. Marketing budgets are tighter, consumers are more skeptical, and social media has changed forever the way we talk about Third-Party Risk Management. How do we gain traction?

<--- Score

120. Who is On the Team?

<--- Score

121. How are we doing compared to our industry?

<--- Score

122. Are we making progress? and are we making progress as Third-Party Risk Management leaders?

<--- Score

123. What counts that we are not counting?

<--- Score

124. What is a good product?

<--- Score

125. What are the business goals Third-Party Risk Management is aiming to achieve?
<--- Score

126. If I had to leave my organization for a year and the only communication I could have with employees was a single paragraph, what would I write?
<--- Score

127. In retrospect, of the projects that we pulled the plug on, what percent do we wish had been allowed to keep going, and what percent do we wish had ended earlier?
<--- Score

128. Is it economical; do we have the time and money?
<--- Score

129. We picked a method, now what?
<--- Score

130. Where can we break convention?
<--- Score

131. To whom do you add value?
<--- Score

132. What does your signature ensure?
<--- Score

133. Do your leaders set clear a direction that is aligned with the vision, mission, and values and is cascaded throughout the organization with measurable goals?
<--- Score

134. If our customer were my grandmother, would I tell her to buy what we're selling?
<--- Score

135. How do we maintain Third-Party Risk Management's Integrity?
<--- Score

136. What are the challenges?
<--- Score

137. How important is Third-Party Risk Management to the user organizations mission?
<--- Score

138. What stupid rule would we most like to kill?
<--- Score

139. What threat is Third-Party Risk Management addressing?
<--- Score

140. Who are four people whose careers I've enhanced?
<--- Score

141. How do we make it meaningful in connecting Third-Party Risk Management with what users do day-to-day?
<--- Score

142. What did we miss in the interview for the worst hire we ever made?
<--- Score

143. How to deal with Third-Party Risk Management Changes?

<--- Score

144. What are strategies for increasing support and reducing opposition?

<--- Score

145. What current systems have to be understood and/or changed?

<--- Score

146. What may be the consequences for the performance of an organization if all stakeholders are not consulted regarding Third-Party Risk Management?

<--- Score

147. Why should people listen to you?

<--- Score

148. How Do We Create Buy-in?

<--- Score

149. Who have we, as a company, historically been when we've been at our best?

<--- Score

150. What would have to be true for the option on the table to be the best possible choice?

<--- Score

151. Who will provide the final approval of Third-Party Risk Management deliverables?

<--- Score

152. What is an unauthorized commitment?
<--- Score

153. If there were zero limitations, what would we do differently?
<--- Score

154. What are your key business, operational, societal responsibility, and human resource strategic challenges and advantages?
<--- Score

155. Do you keep 50% of your time unscheduled?
<--- Score

156. How do you listen to customers to obtain actionable information?
<--- Score

157. Ask yourself: how would we do this work if we only had one staff member to do it?
<--- Score

158. What is the craziest thing we can do?
<--- Score

159. What external factors influence our success?
<--- Score

160. Did my employees make progress today?
<--- Score

161. Is Third-Party Risk Management dependent on the successful delivery of a current project?
<--- Score

162. Which Third-Party Risk Management goals are the most important?

<--- Score

163. Are the criteria for selecting recommendations stated?

<--- Score

164. Has the investment re-baselined during the past fiscal year?

<--- Score

165. What one word do we want to own in the minds of our customers, employees, and partners?

<--- Score

166. How are conflicts dealt with?

<--- Score

167. How will we know when our strategy has been successful?

<--- Score

168. Which models, tools and techniques are necessary?

<--- Score

169. Where is your organization on the performance excellence continuum?

<--- Score

170. How can we become the company that would put us out of business?

<--- Score

171. Do we say no to customers for no reason?

<--- Score

172. How do you govern and fulfill your societal responsibilities?
<--- Score

173. Think about the kind of project structure that would be appropriate for your Third-Party Risk Management project. should it be formal and complex, or can it be less formal and relatively simple?
<--- Score

174. If we got kicked out and the board brought in a new CEO, what would he do?
<--- Score

175. Do we underestimate the customer's journey?
<--- Score

176. How do we foster the skills, knowledge, talents, attributes, and characteristics we want to have?
<--- Score

177. When information truly is ubiquitous, when reach and connectivity are completely global, when computing resources are infinite, and when a whole new set of impossibilities are not only possible, but happening, what will that do to our business?
<--- Score

178. What potential megatrends could make our business model obsolete?
<--- Score

179. How will we build a 100-year startup?
<--- Score

180. In a project to restructure Third-Party Risk Management outcomes, which stakeholders would you involve?
<--- Score

181. What is a feasible sequencing of reform initiatives over time?
<--- Score

182. Are there any disadvantages to implementing Third-Party Risk Management? There might be some that are less obvious?
<--- Score

183. What are your organizations work systems?
<--- Score

184. Who will determine interim and final deadlines?
<--- Score

185. Do we have the right people on the bus?
<--- Score

186. How do senior leaders deploy your organizations vision and values through your leadership system, to the workforce, to key suppliers and partners, and to customers and other stakeholders, as appropriate?
<--- Score

187. How will we know if we have been successful?
<--- Score

188. What is our mission?

<--- Score

189. Are we making progress (as leaders)?

<--- Score

190. What are all of our Third-Party Risk Management domains and what do they do?

<--- Score

191. How much contingency will be available in the budget?

<--- Score

192. How do we engage the workforce, in addition to satisfying them?

<--- Score

193. Do we think we know, or do we know we know ?

<--- Score

194. Who will be responsible for deciding whether Third-Party Risk Management goes ahead or not after the initial investigations?

<--- Score

195. Am I failing differently each time?

<--- Score

196. What are the short and long-term Third-Party Risk Management goals?

<--- Score

197. What trophy do we want on our mantle?

<--- Score

198. Which individuals, teams or departments will be involved in Third-Party Risk Management?
<--- Score

199. What sources do you use to gather information for a Third-Party Risk Management study?
<--- Score

200. Who are the key stakeholders?
<--- Score

201. What management system can we use to leverage the Third-Party Risk Management experience, ideas, and concerns of the people closest to the work to be done?
<--- Score

202. Operational - will it work?
<--- Score

203. If no one would ever find out about my accomplishments, how would I lead differently?
<--- Score

204. What information is critical to our organization that our executives are ignoring?
<--- Score

205. Whom among your colleagues do you trust, and for what?
<--- Score

206. What are specific Third-Party Risk Management

Rules to follow?
<--- Score

207. What is the funding source for this project?
<--- Score

208. Is maximizing Third-Party Risk Management protection the same as minimizing Third-Party Risk Management loss?
<--- Score

209. What are your most important goals for the strategic Third-Party Risk Management objectives?
<--- Score

210. Has implementation been effective in reaching specified objectives?
<--- Score

211. What is Effective Third-Party Risk Management?
<--- Score

212. What have we done to protect our business from competitive encroachment?
<--- Score

213. How much does Third-Party Risk Management help?
<--- Score

214. How do we manage Third-Party Risk Management Knowledge Management (KM)?
<--- Score

215. Who, on the executive team or the board, has spoken to a customer recently?

<--- Score

216. Is there any existing Third-Party Risk Management governance structure?
<--- Score

217. What role does communication play in the success or failure of a Third-Party Risk Management project?
<--- Score

218. Do we have enough freaky customers in our portfolio pushing us to the limit day in and day out?
<--- Score

219. Why don't our customers like us?
<--- Score

220. Whose voice (department, ethnic group, women, older workers, etc) might you have missed hearing from in your company, and how might you amplify this voice to create positive momentum for your business?
<--- Score

221. What is your BATNA (best alternative to a negotiated agreement)?
<--- Score

222. Are we paying enough attention to the partners our company depends on to succeed?
<--- Score

223. Political -is anyone trying to undermine this project?
<--- Score

224. What should we stop doing?
<--- Score

225. How do you determine the key elements that affect Third-Party Risk Management workforce satisfaction? how are these elements determined for different workforce groups and segments?
<--- Score

226. Do you have a vision statement?
<--- Score

227. How do senior leaders set organizational vision and values?
<--- Score

228. What are the Essentials of Internal Third-Party Risk Management Management?
<--- Score

229. Who uses our product in ways we never expected?
<--- Score

230. Instead of going to current contacts for new ideas, what if you reconnected with dormant contacts--the people you used to know? If you were going reactivate a dormant tie, who would it be?
<--- Score

231. What was the last experiment we ran?
<--- Score

232. What new services of functionality will be implemented next with Third-Party Risk

Management ?
<--- Score

Add up total points for this section:
_ _ _ _ _ = Total points for this section

Divided by: _ _ _ _ _ _ (number of
statements answered) = _ _ _ _ _ _
Average score for this section

Transfer your score to the Third-Party
Risk Management Index at the beginning
of the Self-Assessment.

Third-Party Risk Management and Managing Third-Party Risk Management Projects, Criteria for Third-Party Risk Management Project Managers:

Third-Party Risk Management: Communications Management Plan

1. Conflict Resolution -which method when?

2. Who is involved as you identify stakeholders?

3. What is the political influence?

4. Timing: when do the effects of the communication take place?

5. Is there an important stakeholder who is actively opposed and will not receive messages?

6. What approaches do you use?

7. Who to learn from?

8. Are the stakeholders getting the information others need, are others consulted, are concerns addressed?

9. What is Third-Party Risk Management Project Communications Management?

10. What data is going to be required?

11. How often do you engage with stakeholders?

12. What to learn?

13. What help do you and your team need from the stakeholder?

14. Do you have members of your team responsible

for certain stakeholders?

15. Which stakeholders can influence others?

16. What Went Right?

17. Are others needed?

18. What does the stakeholder need from the team?

19. What communications method?

20. Why Manage Stakeholders?

Third-Party Risk Management: Risk Register

21. User Involvement: Do I have the right users?

22. What Went Wrong?

23. What evidence do you have to justify the likelihood score of the risk (audit, incident report, claim, complaints, inspection, internal review)?

24. Risk Documentation: What reporting formats and processes will be used for risk management activities?

25. Technology risk -is the Third-Party Risk Management Project technically feasible?

26. How well are risks controlled?

27. What could prevent us delivering on the strategic program objectives and what is being done to mitigate such issues?

28. What is our current and future risk profile?

29. Have other controls and solutions been implemented in other services which could be applied as an alternative to additional funding?

30. What is a Community Risk Register?

31. What are you going to do to limit the Third-Party Risk Management Projects risk exposure due to the

identified risks?

32. Severity Prediction?

33. People risk -Are people with appropriate skills available to help complete the Third-Party Risk Management Project?

34. Are corrective measures implemented as planned?

35. Assume the risk event or situation happens, what would the impact be?

36. Amongst the action plans and recommendations that you have to introduce are there some that could stop or delay the overall program?

37. What are our key risks/showstoppers and what is being done to manage them?

38. What are the assumptions and current status that support the assessment of the risk?

39. Risk Categories: What are the main categories of risks that should be addressed on this Third-Party Risk Management Project?

Third-Party Risk Management: Third-Party Risk Management Project Schedule

40. To what degree is do you feel the entire team was committed to the Third-Party Risk Management Project schedule?

41. How many levels?

42. Are procedures defined by which the Third-Party Risk Management Project schedule may be changed?

43. Was the Third-Party Risk Management Project schedule reviewed by all stakeholders and formally accepted?

44. Is the Third-Party Risk Management Project schedule available for all Third-Party Risk Management Project team members to review?

45. Schedule/Cost Recovery?

46. It allows the Third-Party Risk Management Project to be delivered on schedule. How Do you Use Schedules?

47. If you can t fix it, how do you do it differently?

48. Your best shot for providing estimations how complex/how much work does the activity require?

49. Change Management Required?

50. Should you include sub-activities?

51. Why Do you Need Schedules?

52. How can you minimize or control changes to Third-Party Risk Management Project schedules?

53. Activity charts and bar charts are graphical representations of a Third-Party Risk Management Project schedule ...how do they differ?

54. Whats the difference?

55. Third-Party Risk Management Project work estimates Who is managing the work estimate quality of work tasks in the Third-Party Risk Management Project schedule?

56. How long does a 12 month Third-Party Risk Management Project take?

57. How can you address that situation?

58. Is the structure for tracking the Third-Party Risk Management Project schedule well defined and assigned to a specific individual?

59. Why is this particularly bad?

Third-Party Risk Management: Quality Management Plan

60. With the Five Whys method, the team considers why the issue being explored occurred. Do others then take that initial answer and ask Why?

61. Does the Third-Party Risk Management Project have a formal Third-Party Risk Management Project Plan?

62. How do you ensure that your sampling methods and procedures meet your data needs?

63. Do the data quality objectives communicate the intended program need?

64. Do you periodically review your data quality system to see that it is up to date and appropriate?

65. Is staff trained on the software technologies that are being used on the Third-Party Risk Management Project?

66. Methodology followed?

67. What are your results for key measures/indicators of accomplishment of organizational strategy?

68. Are best practices and metrics employed to identify issues, progress, performance, etc.?

69. What else should you do now?

70. Contradictory information between different documents?

71. Have all stakeholders been identified?

72. How is staff trained?

73. After observing execution of process, is it in compliance with the documented Plan?

74. Are there processes in place to ensure internal consistency between the source code components?

75. Are there trends or hot spots?

76. How does your organization maintain a safe and healthy work environment?

77. What is the audience for the data?

78. How are deviations from procedures handled?

79. How does the material compare to a regulatory threshold?

Third-Party Risk Management: Initiating Process Group

80. Realistic - Are the desired results expressed in a way that the team will be motivated and believe that the required level of involvement will be obtained?

81. What were the challenges that you encountered during the execution of a previous Third-Party Risk Management Project that you would not want to repeat?

82. Based on your Third-Party Risk Management Project communication management plan, what worked well?

83. Who does what?

84. Were decisions made in a timely manner?

85. What are the constraints?

86. Are stakeholders properly informed about the status of the Third-Party Risk Management Project?

87. Did the Third-Party Risk Management Project team have the right skills?

88. What were things that you need to improve?

89. Which of Six Sigmas DMAIC phases focuses on the measurement of internal process that affect factors that are critical to quality?

90. How do you help others satisfy their needs?

91. The process to Manage Stakeholders is part of which process group?

92. Which Six Sigma DMAIC phase focuses on why and how defects and errors occur?

93. What technical work to do in each phase?

94. What areas were overlooked on this Third-Party Risk Management Project?

95. Did you use a contractor or vendor?

96. How to control and approve each phase?

97. How well did the chosen processes produce the expected results?

98. Do you understand the communication expectations for this Third-Party Risk Management Project?

99. If action is called for, what form should it take?

Third-Party Risk Management: Third-Party Risk Management Project Management Plan

100. How Do you Manage Integration?

101. What are the deliverables?

102. Development trends and opportunities. What if the positive direction and vision of the organization causes expected trends to change?

103. What happened during the process that you found interesting?

104. What does management expect of PMs?

105. Has the selected plan been formulated using cost effectiveness and incremental analysis techniques?

106. Did the planning effort collaborate to develop solutions that integrate expertise, policies, programs, and Third-Party Risk Management Projects across entities?

107. What is the business need?

108. What is Third-Party Risk Management Project Scope Management?

109. What data/reports/tools/etc. do program managers need?

110. Do there need to be organizational changes?

111. Why Do you Manage Integration?

112. When is the Third-Party Risk Management Project management plan created?

113. Are comparable cost estimates used for comparing, screening and selecting alternative plans, and has a reasonable cost estimate been developed for the recommended plan?

114. What are the known stakeholder requirements?

115. If the Third-Party Risk Management Project management plan is a comprehensive document that guides you in Third-Party Risk Management Project execution and control, then what should it NOT contain?

116. How do you manage time?

117. Who Manages Integration?

118. What did not work so well?

Third-Party Risk Management: Schedule Management Plan

119. Are Third-Party Risk Management Project contact logs kept up to date?

120. Does the Third-Party Risk Management Project have a Statement of Work?

121. Are individual tasks of reasonable time effort (8–40 hours)?

122. Are the processes for schedule assessment and analysis defined?

123. Has the business need been clearly defined?

124. Does the detailed Third-Party Risk Management Project plan identify individual responsibilities for the next 4–6 weeks?

125. Why Time Management?

126. What happens if a warning is triggered?

127. Are written status reports provided on a designated frequent basis?

128. Is there a formal process for updating the Third-Party Risk Management Project baseline?

129. Are milestone deliverables effectively tracked and compared to Third-Party Risk Management

Project plan?

130. Is there an issues management plan in place?

131. Does the Resource Management Plan include a personnel development plan?

132. Is there an excessive and invalid use of task constraints and relationships of leads/lags?

133. Have the key elements of a coherent Third-Party Risk Management Project management strategy been established?

134. Where is the scheduling tool and who has access to it to view it?

135. Is there a formal set of procedures supporting Stakeholder Management?

136. Are risk triggers captured?

137. Are metrics used to evaluate and manage Vendors?

138. Has a Quality Assurance Plan been developed for the Third-Party Risk Management Project?

Third-Party Risk Management: Planning Process Group

139. In what way has the program contributed towards the issue culture and development included on the public agenda?

140. If you are late, will anybody notice?

141. How can you make your needs known?

142. Is the identification of the problems, inequalities and gaps, with their respective causes, clear in the Third-Party Risk Management Project?

143. When will the Third-Party Risk Management Project be done?

144. First of all, should any action be taken?

145. Just how important is your work to the overall success of the Third-Party Risk Management Project?

146. Are the follow-up indicators relevant and do they meet the quality needed to measure the outputs and outcomes of the Third-Party Risk Management Project?

147. What should you do next?

148. What types of differentiated effects are resulting from the Third-Party Risk Management Project and to what extent?

149. How well did the chosen processes fit the needs of the Third-Party Risk Management Project?

150. Third-Party Risk Management Project Assessment; Why did you do this Third-Party Risk Management Project?

151. How will it affect you?

152. Have operating capacities been created and/or reinforced in partners?

153. To what extent do the intervention objectives and strategies of the Third-Party Risk Management Project respond to the organizations plans?

154. How does activity resource estimation affect activity duration estimation?

155. What will you do to minimize the impact should a risk event occur?

156. How Will You Know You Did It?

157. Is the schedule for the set products being met?

158. Do the partners have sufficient financial capacity to keep up the benefits produced by the programme?

Third-Party Risk Management: Cost Estimating Worksheet

159. Value Pocket Identification & Quantification What Are Value Pockets?

160. What will others want?

161. What costs are to be estimated?

162. Will the Third-Party Risk Management Project collaborate with the local community and leverage resources?

163. Ask: are others positioned to know, are others credible, and will others cooperate?

164. Identify the timeframe necessary to monitor progress and collect data to determine how the selected measure has changed?

165. Does the Third-Party Risk Management Project provide innovative ways for stakeholders to overcome obstacles or deliver better outcomes?

166. What is the purpose of estimating?

167. What happens to any remaining funds not used?

168. Is the Third-Party Risk Management Project responsive to community need?

169. Is it feasible to establish a control group

arrangement?

170. Who is best positioned to know and assist in identifying such factors?

171. What additional Third-Party Risk Management Project(s) could be initiated as a result of this Third-Party Risk Management Project?

172. Can a trend be established from historical performance data on the selected measure and are the criteria for using trend analysis or forecasting methods met?

173. What info is needed?

174. What Can Be Included?

175. How will the results be shared and to whom?

176. What is the estimated labor cost today based upon this information?

Third-Party Risk Management: Roles and Responsibilities

177. Once the responsibilities are defined for the Third-Party Risk Management Project, have the deliverables, roles and responsibilities been clearly communicated to every participant?

178. Do you take the time to clearly define roles and responsibilities on Third-Party Risk Management Project tasks?

179. Required Skills, Knowledge, Experience?

180. What are my major roles and responsibilities in the area of performance measurement and assessment?

181. How is your work-life balance?

182. Is there a training program in place for stakeholders covering expectations, roles and responsibilities and any addition knowledge others need to be good stakeholders?

183. Influence: What areas of organizational decision making are you able to influence when you do not have authority to make the final decision?

184. Are the quality assurance functions and related roles and responsibilities clearly defined?

185. Who is responsible for each task?

186. Are governance roles and responsibilities documented?

187. Attainable / Achievable: The goal is attainable; can you actually accomplish the goal?

188. Authority: What areas/Third-Party Risk Management Projects in your work do you have the authority to decide upon and act on those decisions?

189. Implementation of actions: Who are the responsible units?

190. What should you do now to prepare yourself for a promotion, increased responsibilities or a different job?

191. Do the values and practices inherent in the culture of the organization foster or hinder the process?

192. Key conclusions and recommendations: Are conclusions and recommendations relevant and acceptable?

193. Have you ever been a part of this team?

194. How well did the Third-Party Risk Management Project Team understand the expectations of specific roles and responsibilities?

195. Are our policies supportive of a culture of quality data?

Third-Party Risk Management: Network Diagram

196. What is the lowest cost to complete this Third-Party Risk Management Project in xx weeks?

197. What are the tools?

198. What are the Major Administrative Issues?

199. If the Third-Party Risk Management Project network diagram cannot change but you have extra personnel resources, what is the BEST thing to do?

200. If a current contract exists, can you provide the vendor name, contract start, and contract expiration date?

201. Will crashing x weeks return more in benefits than it costs?

202. What is the completion time?

203. What is the organization s history in doing similar activities?

204. Can you calculate the confidence level?

205. What to do and When?

206. What can be done concurrently?

207. Why must you schedule milestones, such as

reviews, throughout the Third-Party Risk Management Project?

208. What is the probability of completing the Third-Party Risk Management Project in less that xx days?

209. What job or jobs follow it?

210. What job or jobs precede it?

211. Exercise: What is the probability that the Third-Party Risk Management Project duration will exceed xx weeks?

212. What activities must occur simultaneously with this activity?

213. What activity must be completed immediately before this activity can start?

214. Where do you schedule uncertainty time?

215. What must be completed before an activity can be started?

Third-Party Risk Management: Activity Attributes

216. Where else does it apply?

217. Whats Missing?

218. Activity: Whats In the Bag?

219. Have constraints been applied to the start and finish milestones for the phases?

220. How many days do you need to complete the work scope with a limit of X number of resources?

221. Would you consider either of these activities an outlier?

222. Can you re-assign any activities to another resource to resolve an over-allocation?

223. How difficult will it be to do specific activities on this Third-Party Risk Management Project?

224. Which method produces the more accurate cost assignment?

225. Have you identified the Activity Leveling Priority code value on each activity?

226. Were there other ways you could have organized the data to achieve similar results?

227. Does the organization of the data change its meaning?

228. Is there a trend during the year?

229. Whats the general pattern here?

230. Resource is assigned to?

231. How difficult will it be to complete specific activities on this Third-Party Risk Management Project?

232. Do you feel very comfortable with your prediction?

233. Is there anything planned that doesn t need to be here?

234. Has management defined a definite timeframe for the turnaround or Third-Party Risk Management Project window?

Third-Party Risk Management: Responsibility Assignment Matrix

235. Is the anticipated (firm and potential) business base Third-Party Risk Management Projected in a rational, consistent manner?

236. Are records maintained to show how undistributed budgets are controlled?

237. What is the number one predictor of a group s productivity?

238. Major functional areas of contract effort?

239. Time-phased control account budgets?

240. Budgets assigned to major functional organizations?

241. Are control accounts opened and closed based on the start and completion of work contained therein?

242. What tool can show you individual and group allocations?

243. How many hours by each staff member/rate?

244. What is the purpose of assigning and documenting responsibility?

245. Does each role with Accountable responsibility

have the authority within the organization to make the required decisions?

246. Which resource planning tool provides information on resource responsibility and accountability?

247. Are the overhead pools formally and adequately identified?

248. Does each activity-deliverable have exactly one Accountable responsibility, so that accountability is clear and decisions can be made quickly?

249. The staff interests – is the group or the person interested in working for this Third-Party Risk Management Project?

250. Are there any drawbacks to using a responsibility assignment matrix?

251. Are the organizations and items of cost assigned to each pool identified?

252. Evaluate the performance of operating organizations?

253. When Performing is split among two or more roles, is the work clearly defined so that the efforts are coordinated and the communication is clear?

254. Does the Third-Party Risk Management Project need to be analyzed further to uncover additional responsibilities?

Third-Party Risk Management: Scope Management Plan

255. Timeline and milestones?

256. Are issues raised, assessed, actioned, and resolved in a timely and efficient manner?

257. Are agendas created for each meeting with meeting objectives, meeting topics, invitee list, and action items from past meetings?

258. Have external dependencies been captured in the schedule?

259. Are Third-Party Risk Management Project team members involved in detailed estimating and scheduling?

260. What is the most common tool for helping define the detail?

261. Do you have the reasons why the changes to the organizational systems and capabilities are required?

262. Have adequate procedures been put in place for Third-Party Risk Management Project communication and status reporting across Third-Party Risk Management Project boundaries (for example interdependent software development among interfacing systems)?

263. Are trade-offs between accepting the risk and

mitigating the risk identified?

264. Are Vendor contract reports, reviews and visits conducted periodically?

265. Are actuals compared against estimates to analyze and correct variances?

266. Are enough systems & user personnel assigned to the Third-Party Risk Management Project?

267. What are the risks that could significantly affect the budget of the Third-Party Risk Management Project?

268. What are the risks that could significantly affect the schedule of the Third-Party Risk Management Project?

269. Are corrective actions taken when actual results are substantially different from detailed Third-Party Risk Management Project plan (variances)?

270. What should you drop in order to add something new?

271. Are cause and effect determined for risks when they occur?

272. Are funding resource estimates sufficiently detailed and documented for use in planning and tracking the Third-Party Risk Management Project?

273. Are staffing resource estimates sufficiently detailed and documented for use in planning and tracking the Third-Party Risk Management Project?

Third-Party Risk Management: Resource Breakdown Structure

274. Who delivers the information?

275. The list could probably go on, but, the thing that you would most like to know is, How long & How much?

276. What can you do to improve productivity?

277. What is the organizations history in doing similar activities?

278. When do they need the information?

279. Any Changes from Stakeholders?

280. How should the information be delivered?

281. Changes Based on Input from Stakeholders?

282. What is the number one predictor of a groups productivity?

283. Who is allowed to perform which functions?

284. Who will use the system?

285. What s the difference between % Complete and % work?

286. What Is Third-Party Risk Management Project

Communication Management?

287. How can this help you with team building?

Third-Party Risk Management: Requirements Documentation

288. What is the risk associated with the technology?

289. What are the potential disadvantages/advantages?

290. Who is involved?

291. How will the proposed Third-Party Risk Management Project help?

292. Can you Check System Requirements?

293. Has Requirements Gathering uncovered information that would necessitate changes?

294. How does the proposed Third-Party Risk Management Project contribute to the overall objectives of the organization?

295. What facilities must be supported by the system?

296. What Can Tools Do For Us?

297. Are there legal issues?

298. Is your Business Case still valid?

299. Verifiability. Can the requirements be checked?

300. What is Effective documentation?

301. What happens when requirements are wrong?

302. How can you document system requirements?

303. How does what is being described meet the business need?

304. Does your company restrict technical alternatives?

305. Who provides requirements?

306. What are the acceptance criteria?

307. Have the benefits identified with the system being identified clearly?

Third-Party Risk Management: Milestone List

308. How late can the activity finish?

309. Identify critical paths (one or more) and which activities are on the critical path?

310. What background experience, skills, and strengths does the team bring to the company?

311. Can you derive how soon can the whole Third-Party Risk Management Project finish?

312. Who will manage the Third-Party Risk Management Project on a day-to-day basis?

313. How will you get the word out to customers?

314. Global influences?

315. Sustainable financial backing?

316. Continuity, supply chain robustness?

317. It is to be a narrative text providing the crucial aspects of your Third-Party Risk Management Project proposal answering what, who, how, when and where?

318. Which path is the critical path?

319. Marketing - reach, distribution, awareness?

320. Gaps in capabilities?

321. What date will the task finish?

322. Describe the companys strengths and core competencies. What factors will make the company succeed?

323. Own known vulnerabilities?

324. How soon can the activity finish?

Third-Party Risk Management: Cost Baseline

325. Is the requested change request a result of changes in other Third-Party Risk Management Project(s)?

326. At which frequency ?

327. How will cost estimates be used?

328. Where Do Changes Come From?

329. Who will use such metrics ?

330. Is request in line with priorities?

331. Review your risk triggers -have your risks changed?

332. Why Do you Manage Cost?

333. Has training and knowledge transfer of the operations organization been completed?

334. Has the documentation relating to operation and maintenance of the product(s) or service(s) been delivered to, and accepted by, operations management?

335. Is there anything you need from upper management in order to be successful?

336. Have all approved changes to the schedule baseline been identified and impact on the Third-Party Risk Management Project documented?

337. Has the Third-Party Risk Management Projected annual cost to operate and maintain the product(s) or service(s) been approved and funded?

338. Have all approved changes to the Third-Party Risk Management Project requirement been identified and impact on the performance, cost, and schedule baselines documented?

339. How difficult will it be to do specific tasks on the Third-Party Risk Management Project?

340. How concrete were original objectives?

341. What is the most important thing to do next to make your Third-Party Risk Management Project successful?

342. Does the suggested change request seem to represent a necessary enhancement to the product?

343. How likely is it to go wrong?

344. Definition of done can be traced back to the definitions of what are you providing to the customer in terms of deliverables?

Third-Party Risk Management: WBS Dictionary

345. Incurrence of actual indirect costs in excess of budgets, by element of expense?

346. Changes in the overhead pool and/or organization structures?

347. Should you have a test for each code module?

348. Changes in the current direct and Third-Party Risk Management Projected base?

349. Are data elements summarized through the functional organizational structure for progressively higher levels of management?

350. Are direct or indirect cost adjustments being accomplished according to accounting procedures acceptable to us?

351. Is all budget available as management reserve identified and excluded from the performance measurement baseline?

352. Budgets assigned to control accounts?

353. Is authorization of budgets in excess of the contract budget base controlled formally and done with the full knowledge and recognition of the procuring activity?

354. Identify potential or actual overruns and underruns?

355. Does the contractors system provide for accurate cost accumulation and assignment to control accounts in a manner consistent with the budgets using recognized acceptable costing techniques?

356. What are you counting on?

357. Is work progressively subdivided into detailed work packages as requirements are defined?

358. Where learning is used in developing underlying budgets is there a direct relationship between anticipated learning and time phased budgets?

359. Are the responsibilities and authorities of each of the above organizational elements or managers clearly defined?

360. Are retroactive changes to BCWS and BCWP prohibited except for correction of errors or for normal accounting adjustments?

361. Those responsible for overhead performance control of related costs?

362. Are significant decision points, constraints, and interfaces identified as key milestones?

363. Are indirect costs accumulated for comparison with the corresponding budgets?

Third-Party Risk Management: Stakeholder Analysis Matrix

364. Are the interests in line with the programme objectives?

365. What resources might the stakeholder bring to the Third-Party Risk Management Project?

366. Timescales, deadlines and pressures?

367. Innovative aspects?

368. How affected by the problem(s)?

369. Which resources are required?

370. What are innovative aspects of the organization?

371. Competitive advantages?

372. Alliances: With which other actors is the actor allied, how are they interconnected?

373. Contributions to policy and practice?

374. Who will be affected by the Third-Party Risk Management Project?

375. What unique or lowest-cost resources does the Third-Party Risk Management Project have access to?

376. Who will be responsible for managing the

outcome?

377. What could the organization improve?

378. Technology development and innovation?

379. Who can contribute financial or technical resources towards the work?

380. New technologies, services, ideas?

381. What do you Evaluate?

Third-Party Risk Management: Third-Party Risk Management Project Scope Statement

382. Will the risk documents be filed?

383. Change Management vs. Change Leadership - What's the Difference?

384. Name the 2 elements that deal with providing the detail?

385. Do you anticipate new stakeholders joining the Third-Party Risk Management Project over time?

386. Once its defined, what is the stability of the Third-Party Risk Management Project scope?

387. Why do you need to manage scope?

388. Is the scope of your Third-Party Risk Management Project well defined?

389. Will the Risk Plan be updated on a regular and frequent basis?

390. Was planning completed before the Third-Party Risk Management Project was initiated?

391. Third-Party Risk Management Project Lead, Team Lead, Solution Architect?

392. Will the Risk Status be reported to management

on a regular and frequent basis?

393. If you were to write a list of what should not be included in the scope statement, what are some of the things that you would recommend be described as out-of-scope?

394. Have you been able to thoroughly document the Third-Party Risk Management Projects assumptions and constraints?

395. What actions will be taken to mitigate the risk?

396. Is there an information system for the Third-Party Risk Management Project?

397. What are some of the major deliverables of the Third-Party Risk Management Project?

398. Is the plan under configuration management?

399. Are the meetings set up to have assigned note takers that will add action/issues to the issue list?

400. Will statistics related to QA be collected, trends analyzed, and problems raised as issues?

Third-Party Risk Management: Process Improvement Plan

401. What Lessons Have you Learned So Far?

402. Who should prepare the process improvement action plan?

403. Have the supporting tools been developed or acquired?

404. Does explicit definition of the measures exist?

405. The motive is determined by asking, Why do I want to achieve this goal?

406. What personnel are the champions for the initiative?

407. Are you meeting the quality standards?

408. How Do you Manage Quality?

409. What makes people good SPI coaches?

410. Has the time line required to move measurement results from the points of collection to databases or users been established?

411. Where are you now?

412. What personnel are the change agents for your initiative?

413. Where do you focus?

414. If a Process Improvement Framework Is Being Used, Which Elements Will Help the Problems and Goals Listed?

415. Modeling current processes is great, but will you ever see a return on that investment?

416. Are you following the quality standards?

417. What Actions Are Needed to Address the Problems and Achieve the Goals?

418. What is the return on investment?

419. To elicit goal statements, do you ask a question such as, What do you want to achieve?

420. Why do you want to achieve the goal?

Third-Party Risk Management: Activity List

421. Are the required resources available or need to be acquired?

422. What is the total time required to complete the Third-Party Risk Management Project if no delays occur?

423. How should ongoing costs be monitored to try to keep the Third-Party Risk Management Project within budget?

424. The WBS is developed as part of a Joint Planning session. But how do you know that youve done this right?

425. How will it be performed?

426. In what sequence?

427. When do the individual activities need to start and finish?

428. Who will perform the work?

429. How detailed should a Third-Party Risk Management Project get?

430. What are the critical bottleneck activities?

431. Is infrastructure setup part of your Third-Party

Risk Management Project?

432. What is the least expensive way to complete the Third-Party Risk Management Project within 40 weeks?

433. What is the LF and LS for each activity?

434. When will the work be performed?

435. How do you determine the late start (LS) for each activity?

Third-Party Risk Management: Cost Management Plan

436. Has the schedule been baselined?

437. Are status reports received per the Third-Party Risk Management Project Plan?

438. Were Third-Party Risk Management Project team members involved in the development of activity & task decomposition?

439. Scope of work – What is the scope of work for each of the planned contracts?

440. Are software metrics formally captured, analyzed and used as a basis for other Third-Party Risk Management Project estimates?

441. Are key risk mitigation strategies added to the Third-Party Risk Management Project schedule?

442. Have all involved Third-Party Risk Management Project stakeholders and work groups committed to the Third-Party Risk Management Project?

443. Are all payments made according to the contract(s)?

444. Are all resource assumptions documented?

445. Are adequate resources provided for the quality assurance function?

446. Is there a requirements change management processes in place?

447. Contingency rundown curve be used on the Third-Party Risk Management Project?

448. Have stakeholder accountabilities & responsibilities been clearly defined?

449. Is there an approved case?

450. Is there anything unique in this Third-Party Risk Management Project s scope statement that will affect resources?

451. Does the schedule include Third-Party Risk Management Project management time and change request analysis time?

452. Is it possible to track all classes of Third-Party Risk Management Project work (e.g. scheduled, un-scheduled, defect repair, etc.)?

453. What Strengths do you have?

Third-Party Risk Management: Activity Cost Estimates

454. How do I fund change orders?

455. What is the Third-Party Risk Management Projects sustainability strategy that will ensure Third-Party Risk Management Project results will endure or be sustained?

456. Will you use any tools, such as Third-Party Risk Management Project management software, to assist in capturing Earned Value metrics?

457. The impact and what actions were taken?

458. Are data needed on characteristics of care?

459. What is the estimators estimating history?

460. What is the activity recast of the budget?

461. Who determines the quality and expertise of contractors?

462. Who & what determines the need for contracted services?

463. Performance bond should always provide what part of the contract value?

464. What are the audit requirements?

465. What makes a good expected result statement?

466. Does the activity serve a common type of customer?

467. Was the consultant knowledgeable about the program?

468. How do you change activities?

469. What is included in indirect cost being allocated?

470. What do you want to know about the stay to know if costs were inappropriately high or low?

471. Review – what are some common errors in activities to avoid?

Third-Party Risk Management: Assumption and Constraint Log

472. Was the document/deliverable developed per the appropriate or required standards (for example, Institute of Electrical and Electronics Engineers standards)?

473. Contradictory information between document sections?

474. Have all involved stakeholders and work groups committed to the Third-Party Risk Management Project?

475. Is this model reasonable?

476. Do documented requirements exist for all critical components and areas, including technical, business, interfaces, performance, security and conversion requirements?

477. Have the scope, objectives, costs, benefits and impacts been communicated to all involved and/or impacted stakeholders and work groups?

478. Is the process working, but people are not executing in compliance of the process?

479. Are formal code reviews conducted?

480. Does the document/deliverable meet all requirements (for example, statement of work)

specific to this deliverable?

481. Security analysis has access to information that is sanitized?

482. Have Third-Party Risk Management Project management standards and procedures been established and documented?

483. Does a specific action and/or state that is known to violate security policy occur?

484. Does the system design reflect the requirements?

485. If appropriate, is the deliverable content consistent with current Third-Party Risk Management Project documents and in compliance with the Document Management Plan?

486. Diagrams and tables are included to explain complex concepts and increase overall readability?

Third-Party Risk Management: Activity Duration Estimates

487. What are the main processes included in Third-Party Risk Management Project quality management?

488. Time for overtime?

489. What are two suggestions for ensuring adequate change control on Third-Party Risk Management Projects that involve outside contracts?

490. How is the Third-Party Risk Management Project doing?

491. Is evaluation criteria defined to rate proposals?

492. What type of activity sequencing method is required for these activities?

493. Is a contract developed which obligates the seller and the buyer?

494. Which is the BEST thing to do to try to complete a Third-Party Risk Management Project two days earlier?

495. What are key inputs and outputs of the software?

496. Are activity duration estimates documented?

497. Did anything besides luck make a difference between success and failure?

498. What do you think about the WBSs for them?

499. Are procedures defined by which the Third-Party Risk Management Project scope may be changed?

500. What do you think the real problem was in this case?

501. Do Third-Party Risk Management Project team members work in the same physical location to enhance team performance?

502. Why should Third-Party Risk Management Project managers strive to make their jobs look easy?

503. What is the career outlook for Third-Party Risk Management Project managers in information technology?

504. Do you think many other organizations could apply this methodology, or does each organization need to create its own methodology?

505. Are inspections completed to determine if the results comply with the requirements?

Third-Party Risk Management: Human Resource Management Plan

506. Is there an on-going process in place to monitor Third-Party Risk Management Project risks?

507. Are Vendor invoices audited for accuracy before payment?

508. Were Third-Party Risk Management Project team members involved in detailed estimating and scheduling?

509. Have the key functions and capabilities been defined and assigned to each release or iteration?

510. Is there a set of procedures defining the scope, procedures, and deliverables defining quality control?

511. Are the Third-Party Risk Management Project team members located locally to the users/ stakeholders?

512. Do Third-Party Risk Management Project teams & team members report on status / activities / progress?

513. Are staff skills known and available for each task?

514. Does the Business Case include how the Third-Party Risk Management Project aligns with the organizations strategic goals & objectives?

515. Have the procedures for identifying budget

variances been followed?

516. Are post milestone Third-Party Risk Management Project reviews (PMPR) conducted with the organization at least once a year?

517. Have process improvement efforts been completed before requirements efforts begin?

518. Do Third-Party Risk Management Project managers participating in the Third-Party Risk Management Project know the Third-Party Risk Management Projects true status first hand?

519. Are parking lot items captured?

520. How well does the company communicate?

Third-Party Risk Management: Activity Resource Requirements

521. When does Monitoring Begin?

522. Anything else?

523. What is the Work Plan Standard?

524. How many signatures do you require on a check and does this match what is in your policy and procedures?

525. Which logical relationship does the PDM use most often?

526. Why do you do that?

527. Do you use tools like decomposition and rolling-wave planning to produce the activity list and other outputs?

528. What are constraints that you might find during the Human Resource Planning process?

529. Organizational Applicability?

530. Are there unresolved issues that need to be addressed?

531. Other support in specific areas?

532. How do you handle petty cash?

Third-Party Risk Management: Third-Party Risk Management Project Charter

533. Run it as as a startup?

534. Is it an improvement over existing products?

535. Where and How Does the Team Fit Within the Organization Structure?

536. What ideas do you have for initial tests of change (PDSA cycles)?

537. How are Third-Party Risk Management Projects different from Operations?

538. What does it need to do?

539. Avoid costs, improve service, and/ or comply with a mandate?

540. Who is the sponsor?

541. Rough time estimate 2 months or 2 yrs?

542. Are you building in-house ?

543. Customer Benefits: What customer requirements does this Third-Party Risk Management Project address?

544. Why have you chosen the aim you have set forth?

545. Major High-Level Milestone Targets: What events measure progress?

546. For whom?

547. What are you trying to accomplish?

548. What are the assumptions?

549. What's in it for you?

Third-Party Risk Management: Quality Metrics

550. What approved evidence based screening tools can be used?

551. How should customers provide input?

552. What does this tell us?

553. What are the organizations expectations for its quality Third-Party Risk Management Project?

554. Has risk analysis been adequately reviewed?

555. What can manufacturing professionals do to ensure quality is seen as an integral part of the entire product lifecycle?

556. Are there any open risk issues?

557. Have alternatives been defined in the event that failure occurs?

558. Do the operators focus on determining; is there anything I need to worry about?

559. Is the reporting frequency appropriate?

560. Can visual measures help us to filter visualizations of interest?

561. Who is willing to lead?

562. Is there a set of procedures to capture, analyze and act on quality metrics?

563. How do you communicate results and findings to upper management?

564. The metrics–whats being considered?

565. What happens if you get an abnormal result?

566. What about still open problems?

567. Was material distributed on time?

568. How do you measure?

569. Do you know how much profit a 10% decrease in waste would generate?

Third-Party Risk Management: Third-Party Risk Management Project Portfolio management

570. What are the four types of portfolios on which a PMO must focus?

571. If the PMO does not properly balance the portfolio of Third-Party Risk Management Projects, who will?

572. What Happens without Third-Party Risk Management Project Portfolio and Proper Resourcing?

573. Are you working differently with your portfolios at different parts of the organization?

574. How does the organization ensure that Third-Party Risk Management Project and program benefits and risks are being managed to optimize the overall value creation from the portfolio?

575. Why should the resource portfolio contain a minimum of information?

576. Regularly review and revise the Third-Party Risk Management Project portfolio (eg several times a year) are done?

577. Do you have a risk-based approach to portfolio management?

578. Agility. How do organizations re-align portfolio when strategic objectives change?

579. Why would the Governance Board want to know the current portfolio opportunity?

580. Governance. How does the organization ensure that Third-Party Risk Management Project and program benefits and risks are being managed to optimize the overall value creation from the portfolio?

581. The portfolio management process force ranks work based on known strategic direction; What do you want to achieve strategically for the current and subsequent fiscal years?

582. Consider the benefit of the strategic objectives portfolio and its relationship to the Third-Party Risk Management Project portfolio. How is this helpful in Third-Party Risk Management Project selection?

583. Are portfolios aligned to strategic business objectives?

584. How do organizations re-align portfolio when strategic objectives change?

585. What are the four types of portfolios a PMO must focus on?

586. Strategic fit. Are portfolios aligned to strategic business objectives?

587. Do you analyse the impact of individual new Third-Party Risk Management Projects to the overall portfolio?

588. How much information about an asset do you think a PMO needs to develop its asset portfolio?

589. Have regular Third-Party Risk Management Project portfolio reporting?

Third-Party Risk Management: Risk Management Plan

590. Are the best people available?

591. Does the customer understand the software process?

592. Are staff committed for the duration of the product?

593. Risks should be identified during which phase of Third-Party Risk Management Project management life cycle?

594. Is the process being followed?

595. Can the Third-Party Risk Management Project proceed without assuming the risk?

596. Are formal technical reviews part of this process?

597. Costs associated with late delivery or a defective product?

598. Could others have been better mitigated?

599. Is the process supported by tools?

600. Do you have a mechanism for managing change?

601. Financial risk -can the organization afford to undertake the Third-Party Risk Management Project?

602. What is the impact to the Third-Party Risk Management Project if the item is not resolved in a timely fashion?

603. What things might go wrong?

604. Are the reports useful and easy to read?

605. Can the risk be avoided by choosing a different alternative?

606. How risk averse are you?

Third-Party Risk Management: Requirements Management Plan

607. After the requirements are gathered and set forth on the requirements register, they're little more than a laundry list of items. Some may be duplicates, some might conflict with others and some will be too broad or too vague to understand. Describe how the requirements will be analyzed. Who will perform the analysis?

608. Do you really need to write this document at all?

609. Is the Change Control process documented?

610. Will you use an assessment of the Third-Party Risk Management Project environment as a tool to discover risk to the requirements process?

611. To see if a requirement statement is sufficiently well-defined, read it from the developer's perspective. Mentally add the phrase, "call me when you're done" to the end of the requirement and see if that makes you nervous. In other words, would you need additional clarification from the author to understand the requirement well enough to design and implement it?

612. Who will initially review the Third-Party Risk Management Project work or products to ensure it meets the applicable acceptance criteria?

613. Is there formal agreement on who has authority

to request a change in requirements?

614. How will you develop the schedule of requirements activities?

615. How will requirements be managed?

616. Do you know which stakeholders will participate in the requirements effort?

617. Are actual resource expenditures versus planned still acceptable?

618. Is the system software (non-operating system) new to the IT Third-Party Risk Management Project team?

619. Will the Third-Party Risk Management Project requirements become approved in writing?

620. Who will perform the analysis?

621. Who will approve the requirements (and if multiple approvers, in what order)?

622. Is it new or replacing an existing business system or process?

623. Is stakeholder risk tolerance an important factor for the requirements process in this Third-Party Risk Management Project?

624. Which hardware or software, related to, or as outcome of the Third-Party Risk Management Project is new to the organization?

625. Do you have price sheets and a methodology for determining the total proposal cost?

Third-Party Risk Management: Requirements Traceability Matrix

626. Do we have a clear understanding of all subcontracts in place?

627. Will you use a Requirements Traceability Matrix?

628. Are Third-Party Risk Management Project requirements stable?

629. What percentage of Third-Party Risk Management Projects are producing traceability matrices between requirements and other work products?

630. What is the WBS?

631. Is there a requirements traceability process in place?

632. How small is small enough?

633. Describe the process for approving requirements so they can be added to the traceability matrix and Third-Party Risk Management Project work can be performed. Will the Third-Party Risk Management Project requirements become approved in writing?

634. Why Do you Manage Scope?

635. How Do you Manage Scope?

636. What is out anticipated volatility of the requirements?

637. Why use a WBS?

638. How will it affect the stakeholders personally in their career?

639. What are the chronologies, contingencies, consequences, criteria?

Third-Party Risk Management: Duration Estimating Worksheet

640. Why Estimate Costs?

641. How can the Third-Party Risk Management Project be displayed graphically to better visualize the activities?

642. When, then?

643. What is your role?

644. What is Cost and Third-Party Risk Management Project Cost Management?

645. Can the Third-Party Risk Management Project be constructed as planned?

646. Do any colleagues have experience with the company and/or RFPs?

647. When does the organization expect to be able to complete it?

648. What s an Average Third-Party Risk Management Project?

649. What questions do you have?

650. Small or Large Third-Party Risk Management Project?

651. Done before proceeding with this activity or what can be done concurrently?

652. For other activities, how much delay can be tolerated?

653. What work will be included in the Third-Party Risk Management Project?

Third-Party Risk Management: Stakeholder Register

654. What are the major Third-Party Risk Management Project milestones requiring communications or providing communications opportunities?

655. What is the power of the stakeholder?

656. How Big is the Gap?

657. Who wants to talk about Security?

658. How will Reports Be Created?

659. How should employers make their voices heard?

660. What & Why?

661. Who is Managing Stakeholder Engagement?

662. How much influence do they have on the Third-Party Risk Management Project?

663. Who are the stakeholders?

664. What opportunities exist to provide communications?

665. Is Your Organization Ready for Change?

Index

CPSIA information can be obtained
at www.ICGtesting.com
Printed in the USA
BVHW040159260119
538755BV00018B/412/P